RIEAeuropa Concept Series
Editor: Lebbeus Woods

Sotirios Kotoulas
SPACE OUT
c/o RIEA (Research Institute for Experimental Architecture)
Europa, Bern, Switzerland

Printed in Austria

Springer Wien New York is a part of
Springer Science + Business Media
springeronline.com

Printing: A. Holzhausen Druck & Medien GmbH, 1140 Wien, Österreich

Printed on acid-free and chlorine-free bleached paper

With numerous illustrations

SPIN: 11383338
CIP data applied for

ISSN 1610-0719
ISBN 10 3-211-24488-3 Springer Wien New York
ISBN 13 978-3-211-24488-3 Springer Wien New York

Editor
Lebbeus Woods

Photography
Tina Tyrell, Sotirios Kotoulas

Graphic design
H1reber, büro destruct, Bern, 2005

To my friend, the late architect, Dr. Dimitrios N. Styliaras.

Acknowledgements
Lebbeus Woods, for his trust and support. Anthony Vidler, Anders Abraham, Sean Sculley, Dwayne Oyler. Nicholas Kotoulas for sharing his knowledge of outer space. Konstantine, Chrysoula and Voula Kotoulas, Zab, H1, David Marold, Guy Lafranchi, Tina Tyrell, Larry Newitt and the Geomagnetic Laboratory, Ottawa. Natural Resources Canada, Government of Canada. Edward Atkinson and the Department of Culture, Language, Elders and Youth, Government of Nunavut, Igloolik. World Data Centre for Geomagnetism, Kyoto. Hudson Bay Company Archives, Archives of Manitoba, Winnipeg. National Film Board of Canada, Montreal. On the next level: Alex Kwartler, Jonah Corne, John Shimkus, Rafael Bauer, Paul Granger, Konstantine Papadimitricopoulos, Nikos Katsaounis, Guy Spyropoulos.

This work was made during the spring semester of 2003 at The Cooper Union.
Maps 1 though 6: 38"x38" graphite on cotton paper.
Construction: basswood: 96"x$10^{1/2}$"x 22".
Photographs: Tina Tyrell (cover, 76, 78, 79, 80, 82, 83, 94, 95).

p. 8 "Crossing Boothia Peninsula, April, 1926."
HBCA Photographs 1987/363-D-19/50(N15730)

p. 9 "Building snow-houses on trail from Frobisher Bay to Lake Harbour in 1918" Photographer: J. Cantley
HBCA Photographs 1987/363-E-400/56(N15731)

p. 12,13 "Regiones Sub Polo Arctico" By J. Blaeu. 50 x 68 cm; 20"x $23^{3/4}$"
HBCA Maps G.3/48

p. 24 [Sketch map of the routes between Cumberland House and Split Lake 'Drawn by Cha chay pay way ti May 1806']. In Peter Fidler's Journal of Exploration. 23.2x36.8 cm; $9^{1/4}$ "x$14^{1/2}$"
HBCA Maps E.3/4 fo. 13d (N3354)

p. 25 [Sketch maps 'Drawn by Thoo ool del 29th April 1809' of routes from 'Athapescow Lake' to 'Sea Coast'] (top). Iskemo sketch [coast line from Churchill to Chesterfield Inlet 'Drawn by Nay hek til lok an Iskemo 40 years of age, 8th July 1809'] (lower). Redrawn by Peter Fidler.
HBCA Maps E.3/4 fo. 16 (N6479)

p. 30 Operational Navigation Chart, New York Public Library, ONC A-0, 1980.

p. 32 A large sunspot group photographed on May 17, 1951. (Photograph from Mount Wilson and Las Campanas Observatories), Courtesy of the Observatories of the Carnegie Institute of Washington.

p. 33 [From 'The Sunspot-Activity in the Years 1610–1960 by M. Waldmeier. Schultess & Co. Zurich [1961]: courtesy of M. Waldmeier.]

p. 44 Magnetic Declination Chart of Canada 2000. Natural Resources Canada, Geological survey of Canada.

SOTIRIOS KOTOULAS

Born in Winnipeg, Canada.
Studied piano, theory and harmony with the Royal Conservatory of Music of Toronto, (1984-1998).
Educated in Architecture at The Cooper Union (1998-2003).
Received the Abraham E. Kazan award for Urban Design Studies.
He designed and followed the construction of a house for his family in Winnipeg (1996-2001).
Guest critic at architecture schools in Canada, Europe and the United States.
His work has been published in several architectural journals and televised on the Canadian Broadcasting Corporation.
The Forum House proposal received the Prix de Public from the citizens of Winnipeg (2004).
He is currently designing a house on the island of Seriphos, Greece.
Lives in New York City.

Crossing Boothia Peninsula, April, 1926.

Building snow-houses on trail from Frobisher Bay to Lake Harbour in 1918. Photographer: J. Cantley.

Editor's introduction

It is rare to encounter basic research in the field of architecture, but this publication gives us a chance to do so. By its nature, basic research opens up new and unfamiliar domains that address the foundations of our knowledge. Architects, absorbed as they are in contemporary problems of design, devote little time to questioning the assumptions underlying their work. What is space? How do we know it? What constitutes its reality, its physical fabric? What material forces lying beyond the realm of the visual shape the physicality of space and human comprehension of it?
Our present world is greatly impacted by the invisible, and most extensively by a focus of the author's research, electromagnetic forces. Computers and the internet, satellites and cell phones, indeed, all of the electronic instrumentation our globally interconnected civilization increasingly relies upon for cohesion, engage the range of an electromagnetic spectrum of which visible light is but a sliver. In a palpable sense, we already inhabit electromagnetic space and are part of its constituency, as the term 'cyberspace' attempts to acknowledge. The reason we do not know where cyberspace is, or when we are in it, or how it looks and feels when we are is because our conceptual and perceptual faculties are stuck in older ideas of space. We are hemmed in by our present assumptions and by our inability to visualize, and thus physically experience, space that we cannot measure by means we already know. The author aims to change this by bringing the invisible into the realm of the visible. Without losing his sense of awe, or reducing the immeasurable, he accomplishes his mission by traveling to polar regions of the far north, to the geographical edges, if not the metaphysical limits, of our present civilization, where the visual dimension of our experience is distorted by extreme conditions. He recognizes it as a chance to not only extend our knowledge of ourselves and what we create, but to add something new to the apparatus of our understanding. His is a polar expedition of the mind, and the territories – conceptual and physical – his rigorous and imaginative explorations reveal are claimed by him, quite appropriately, in the name of architecture.

Lebbeus Woods

REGIONES
SVB POLO ARCTICO.
Auctore Guiljelmo Blaeu.
FRIGVS iners illic habitant, Pallorque, Tremorq;
Et jejuna FAMES.
New South Wales.
Buttons Bay
New North Wales.
James his Bay.
NOVA BRITANNIA.
Baffins Bay.
Fretum Hudson
FRETVM DAVIS
Terra de Corterealis
TERRA NOVA
YSLANDIA
OCEANV
SEPTEN
TRIONALIS.
Linea sub Circulo Arctico.
Amplissimo Spectatissimo Prudentissimo Viro
GVILIELMO BACKER DE CORNELIIS,
Reip. Amstelodamensis Consuli et Senatori, nec non in Consessu Societatis Indiae Orientalis Assessori Tabulam hanc D.D. Joh. Blaeu.

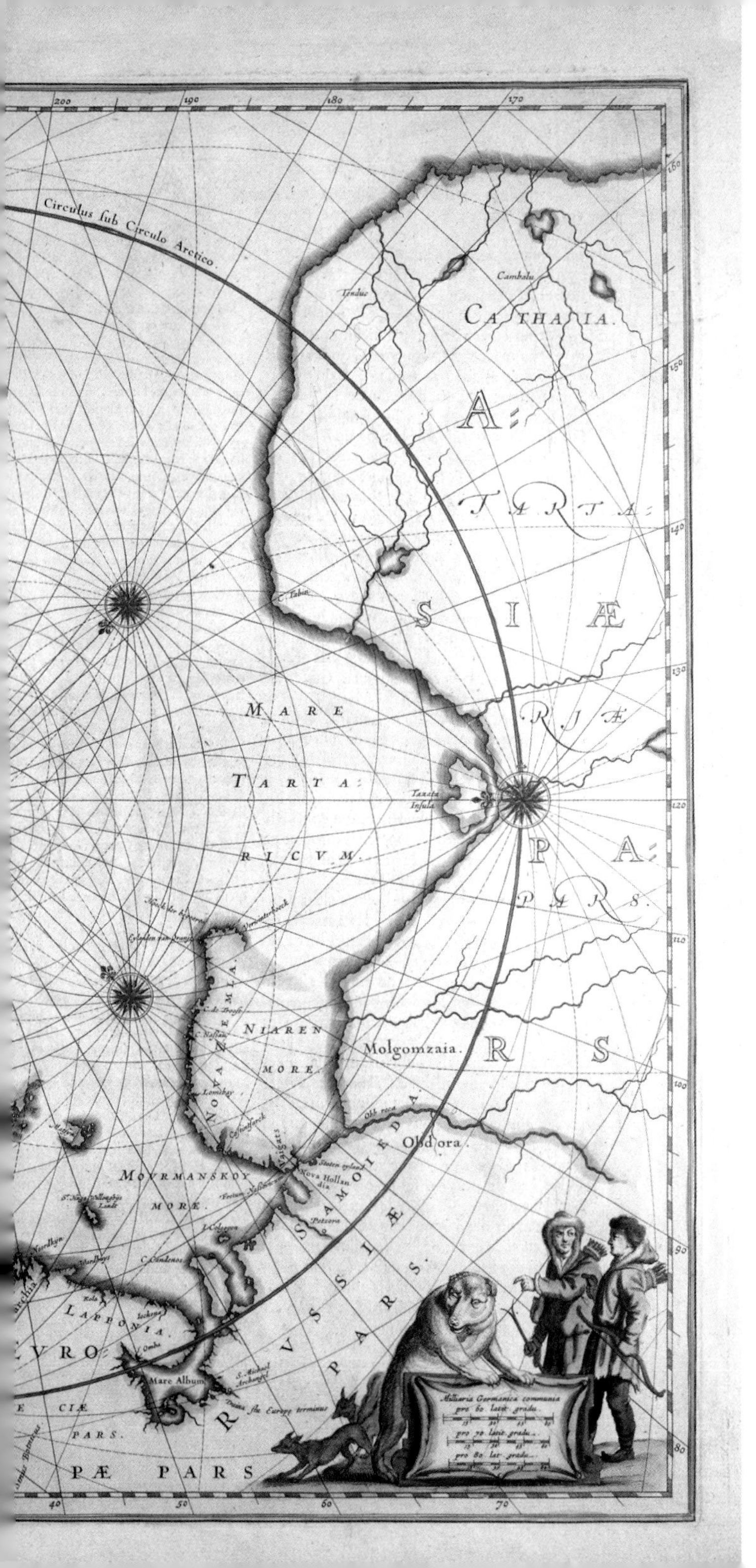

Regiones Sub Polo Arctico c. 1650,
J. Blaeu, cartographer

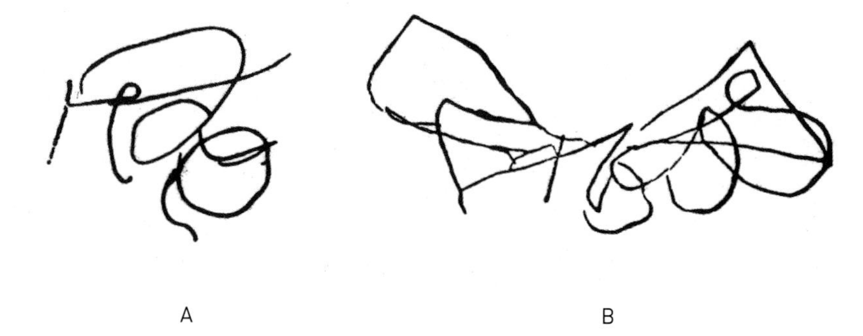

Necromancy. In his salon, Baron L. de Güldenstubbe evoked the dead to write with a pencil directly on a blank piece of paper. The invisible force of the exhumed corpse moved the pencil. These are writings transferred from the objectless realm.
Image: L. de Güldenstubbe, Pneumatologie positive et experimentale Paris, 1857

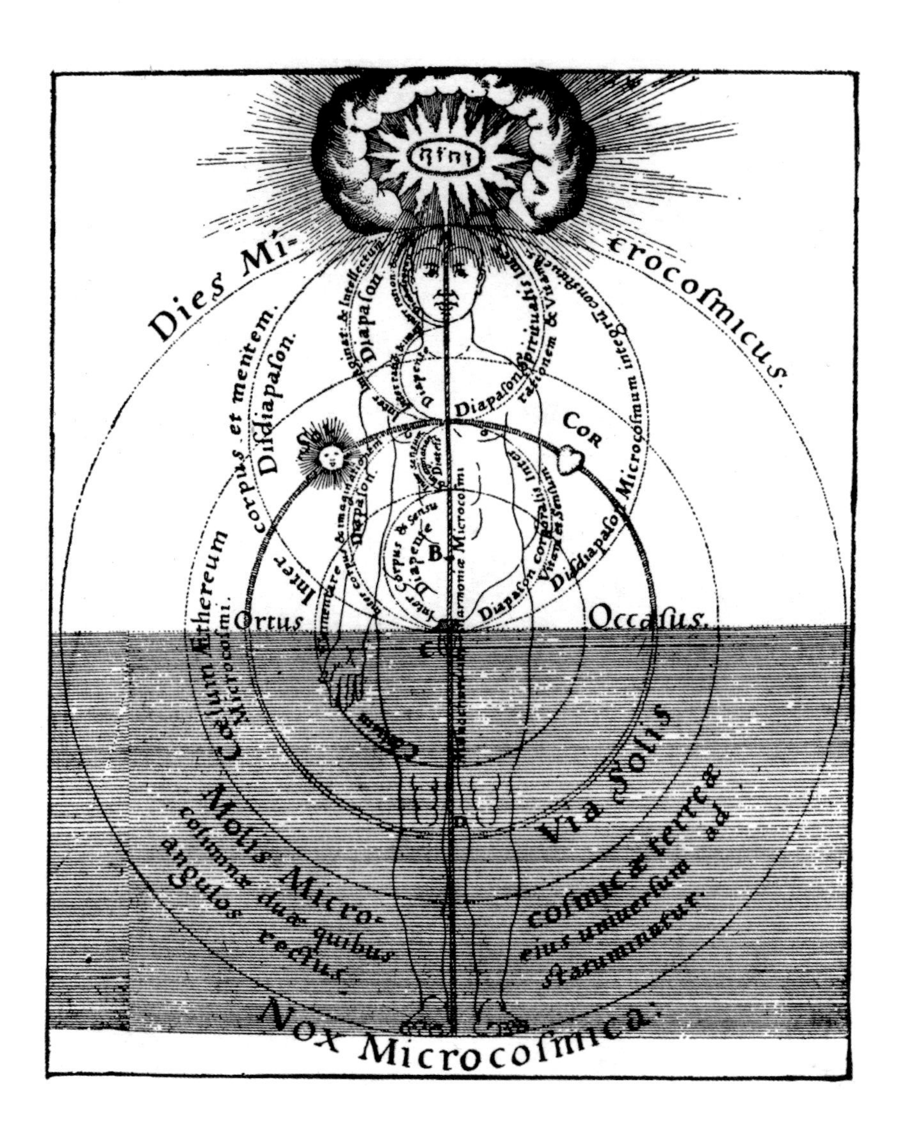

Robert Fludd, The Day and Night of the Microcosm. In this image the scale of the body and the cosmos are harmonically related. Based on musical intervals and star paths, Robert Fludd projects the phenomenon of day and night onto the body. The celestial solar system causes day and night on earth, similarly day and night are located in the body's organs, to determine day and night in man. The upper body is day and the lower body is night.

This book records the process of fabricating an architecture derived from what we cannot see. Through scale, a hallucination distinguishes the immeasurable homogeneous landscape above the Arctic Circle. Invisible electromagnetic phenomena confront the limits of the body to establish a scalar threshold with the celestial. This is not an inhabitable site-specific architecture; rather, it is translatable— existing outside the realm of building as an architecture about architecture.

There exists a mutual influence between the Heavenly bodies, the Earth and Animate Bodies...the phenomena of electricity and magnetism.
Dr. Franz Mesmer [1]

The horror of it was that I was nothing but a line, In normal life one is a sphere, a sphere that surveys panoramas.
Henri Michaux [2]

This fruition of the visible in the invisible for which we are responsible, is the very task of dying...In the world things are transformed into objects in order to be grasped, utilized, made more certain in the distinct rigor of their limits and the affirmation of a homogeneous and divisible space. But in imaginary space things are transformed into that which cannot be grasped. Out of use, beyond wear, they are not in our possession but are the movement of dispossession which releases us both from them and from ourselves...into a place where nothing retains us at all.
Maurice Blanchot [3]

ELECTROMAGNETIC VISION

Above the Arctic Circle, the solstice denies twilight's mixtures of light and dark and produces a continuous day of black or white. These solar days reach the pure origins of illumination over six months, dissolving one another day after day in fog, dissipating the landscape into a pure, continuous, flat, blank black/white out, dense, indifferent and limitless. The migrating Magnetic North Pole attracts particles from the magnetic fields of the sun and the earth, joining many forces from different origins in an anomaly. At a regional scale the electrical fields shift according to the strength of the fluid molten nickel and iron within the earth's core and the old magnetic forces caught in igneous rocks at the surface. At a greater scale, resistance diminishes as electric currents no longer separate these fields but reconnect them in a magnetized plasma. The particles of the protective magnetosphere do not collide and produce zero resistance. However, at a micro scale anomalous resistance will break the magnetic field lines and scatter the particles. Where the two magnetic fields intersect, particle and field energy from space enter the earth's magnetic field where it is collected and released as a substorm. Approximately six substorms occur each day. Multiple substorms create a magnetic storm capable of shifting the electric currents and boundaries of a magnetic field. All optical phenomena are restless electromagnetic particles and waves having zero mass. At moments the strength of an electromagnetic field can overcome the force of gravity. The fields meet in hallucinatory space, usually inside a zone one kilometre above the planet's surface.

DECENTRALIZE

Electricity and magnetism bind the celestial and terrestrial zones through a body no longer defined by its physical structure. By the flowing electromagnetic solution the result is an "ebb and flow" that spans a great scalar interval. In his thesis on "The influence of planets on the human body," Dr. Mesmer writes of the effects of an "all penetrating fluid" produced by the sun and moon on the "parts" that make up the animate body, specifically the receptive nervous system. This substance penetrates everything through the "intensification and remission of the properties of matter and organic bodies--such as gravity, cohesion, elasticity, irritability, electricity." [4] It sets off a cycle that could be measured and harnessed. To heal his patients he simulated an electromagnetic "ebb and flow" to link a body part or organ to a cosmic field by applying magnets to specific body parts, an arrangement he compares to the binding of the sun, moon and oceans which cause tides. Phenomena find meaning in existing forces; the body is defined by the flows of electromagnetism and the visual effects they produce within the nervous system and the mind. The expanded universal field fragments the body across multiple fields. Territories disband where space cannot memorize the physical body. A hollowed body receives the lines; it is encased in its ante-rooms, in the spaces of memory.

LINES

Attracted by the earth's magnetic poles, sun spot emissions of an electron/proton plasma (solar wind) pour into the atmosphere with an electromagnetic force that renders instruments useless. Magnetism and radiation interrupt mechanical and electronic communication and navigational systems, damaging spacecraft and disrupting central power supplies. To navigate a polar magnetic landscape with unreliable instruments requires a construction of an artificial horizon that determines measurements, divides the particular from the immeasurable and defines an unstable geometric origin. A series of maps acting as instruments bring the phenomena back to our scale and guide the navigator through the unpredictable landscape. The maps are like nets stretched across the landscape catching instants of anomalous qualities and quantities outside the visible spectrum: radio, infrared, ultraviolet, gamma and x-rays.

The twilight disappears to form total light and total dark, and the hallucinations begin at 0 degrees centigrade. As the Arctic ocean melts and fluctuates between its states of solid and liquid, it simultaneously melts and freezes to form a direction-less infinite threshold. The Magnetic North Pole shifts the geographic lines of longitude and latitude, which bend, break and dissipate along the landscape, revealing moments at impossible coordinates. The paradoxical space of polar magnetism suggests the possibility of inhabiting a space with no background or foreground, where figures cannot separate themselves from the field, to form something coherent. The body inhabits the point and the line.

CHAIN

With depth, perception dissipates measurable space into a series of remnants suspended in the limitless. Edgar Allen Poe describes this as the "most unconceivable expanse of space- a shadowy and fluctuating domain, now shrinking, now swelling, with the vacillating energies of imagination." [5] A hallucination only develops in diminished consciousness. When full clear visual consciousness attempts to take hold of it or 'grasp' it, it quickly disappears. Injecting himself with a dose of mescaline, Sartre experienced a hallucination that began with a voice singing in a nearby room. Drawn to it, he began to approach the room only to be interrupted by the appearance of "three small parallel clouds" [6] in front of him. He immediately tried to grasp them and that made everything disappear. Hallucinations cannot confront "personal" consciousness because they are autonomous others, they are doubles or multiple species emanating from the one they drain; "their essence is to be ungraspable...they are the words one hears but cannot listen to, the faces one sees but cannot look at." [7] Sartre locates the moment of hallucination in perceptual space, defining it as the "sudden annihilation of perceived reality," [8] producing "a vision situated in a space that is not in its essence the visual." The hallucinations only appear beyond or behind observation in an "unstructured consciousness," where subjects and objects temporarily disappear. They swiftly rebuild in the personal consciousness as the hallucinist, horrified and shocked by the unexpected and absurd hallucination, repeats the memory to form the image. The hallucinatory event is experienced after the event in a synthesis of fragmented memories combining past and future time variables which construct an idea of a whole. [9] The exceedingly possessive nature of the hallucinatory state exhausts and substitutes the first person for the third; "concentrat[ing] his attention on a single detail, to forget himself sufficiently to bring the desired hallucination and so substitute the vision of a reality for the reality itself." [10] Emptiness must not be filled with thoughts or objects from another origin. It must be kept empty by filling it with different contradictions from the same origin. The arctic whiteout induces the hallucinations that fill the emptiness.

PULLOUT

Scale—climbing defines and measures the fields of points that perforate the outside, providing micro data to fragment the uniform expanse. Limitations of scale diversify a phenomenon into a series of contradictory relations: the body as an origin of scale is defined as a corpse, as a living and dead body, limited by the vertical and horizontal data. In the field, the body is released from these data and the limits of gravity, threatening its stability with the forces that are too weak to sense and too strong to engage. The dissolution of distance and size gives way to depth and the objectless states of perception and hallucination. A hallucination (παραισθηση) is the feeling and sensing of what is near and beyond us. The momentary absence of an external object stimulates a vision of an infinitely expanding landscape without any scalar relation to the body. The form of the hallucination is a "sudden rapid event, like a flash, which then yields to the impetuous, elementary force of sensorial reality which requires no verification." [11] While it is momentarily occupying measurable space as a suspended anterior space, behind, in front, before and after measurable space, revealing an anomaly of the space, it is simultaneously constructed of disappearances. The hallucination scatters dimensions but retains the ability to limit the invisible through restless paradoxical proportions, sensible as they pass through measurable space, separating time from the space they momentarily inhabit.

Anterior space enters matter: landscapes, objects, animals, atmospheres and bodies and transforms them according to their physical properties and the surrounding electromagnetic conditions. The temporary union is plural, it is malleable, fragile, viscous and receptive to the innumerable 'voices' it hears; it sets out to break down the monolithic. This architecture develops in reflexive cycles where the regional periodically rises to engage the celestial and define the various invisible scales from which a tangible construction emanates.

LANDSLIDE

The arctic tundra is a treeless cold plain where lichens, grasses, mosses, sedges and low shrubs tend to grow in dark wet soils. Permafrost never recedes and evaporation rates are low, so moisture tends to pool. The pine trees growing near the edge of the tundra embody the disproportionality of the corporal and celestial scales. A fully-grown tree here is about 4 feet tall, however it is proportionally equal in dimension to a fully-grown pine tree in its native location. These trees expand the landscape by changing the relative scale, compressing the ground against the atmosphere to construct summit space. Here the body confronts an unbalanced scale, tipped by an expanding atmosphere proportionally contracting the landscape; it keeps us out when in fact we are inside.

WHITE NIGHT

In the white out and under the effects of the magnetic north pole, a navigator encounters a coordinate volume where readings throughout a territory are the same; the point swells to become a volume. Having lost his bearings, the navigator is everywhere at once; he moves but his location does not change;

volumes of one coordinate find themselves temporarily inside another coordinate, points within points, a dark space in the day. In this dark space, telemetric hallucinations clear a space for the navigator: 1:1 with the immeasurable. At points above or on the earth's surface, anomalies are recorded as vectors imbued with magnitude and direction in three-dimensional space. Intersections of time shift scale, influencing hallucinations of a closed invisible outside. All is killed when drawn.

MISPLACE

Dr. Wilder Penfield induced patients with hallucinations by directly stimulating parts of the brain with a mild electric current. After administering a local anaesthetic, part of the skull was removed and an electric current was introduced to the brain causing the conscious patient to have an "altered interpretation of the present experience," while at times "everything might seem suddenly familiar or farther away or nearer." [12] Some patients were able to recall the memory of an 'aura' like state preceding their seizure. In successful cases, the recalled memory aroused the same emotions, sensations and thoughts experienced during the hallucination preceding the seizure, allowing Dr. Penfield to accurately locate the origin of the seizure on the brain and repair the damaged tissue. Hallucinations were only induced by a stimulation of the temporal lobes at the cerebral cortex, where memory, perceptual awareness, thinking, comprehension, language and consciousness function. The patients recognized the re-occurring past as "authentic," as the stimulation reduced everything to an elementary translation of prior memory. For instance, when the visual cortex was stimulated the patients saw "flickering lights," "colours," "stars," "wheels," "blue green and red coloured disks," "fawn and blue lights," " coloured balls whirling," "radiating grey spots becoming pink and blue," "a long white mark," "shadow moving," "black wheel" [13] and so on.

NECTAR

The hallucinaton expands the imaginary to mediate, transport and translate the "beyond" through fiction. Developing its own language (point, line, plane), it renders an architecture behind architecture that embodies the essence, substance, meaning and form of the anomalous phenomenon. This impossible space is based on scientific data. The intersection translates the invisible substances underlying phenomena into an image of their death. Blanchot describes the corpse as the thing we cannot locate because "death suspends the relation to place" and so in its presence a relationship between "here and nowhere" [14] is grasped. The dead are "behind the world," outside, in a state of placelessness, haunting us because they are "something inaccessible from which we cannot extricate ourselves." [15] At moments, the homogeneity of the arctic landscape brings the nowhere to consciousness and assigns a fictional coordinate to it. An architecture restricting space to the mechanical properties and dimensions of the material body neglects to recognize the existing periodic transmissions between the mind and the landscape, which often produce illogical conditions that challenge habits and provoke the rituals involved in inhabitation.

[1] *Mesmerism* (Los Altos, California: George Bloch, 1980), p. 67.
[2] *Miserable Miracle* (New York: New York Review Books, 2002), p. 126
[3] *The Space of Literature* (Lincoln, NE: University of Nebraska Press), p. 141.
[4] *Mesmerism*, p. 46.
[5] *Eureka* (London: Hesperus Press Ltd., 2002), p. 19.
[6] Sartre, Jean-Paul, *The Imaginary* (New York: Routledge, 2004), p. 156.
[7] Ibid, p. 157.
[8] Ibid, p.150.
[9] Ibid, p. 156, 157
[10] Huysman, Joris K., *Against Nature* (New York, Penguin, 2001), p. 22.
[11] Minkowski, Eugene, *Lived Time; phenomenological and psychopathological studies* (Evanston, IL: Northwestern University Press, 1970), p. 420.
[12] Penfield, Wilder, and Lamar Roberts. *Speech and Brain Mechanisms* (Princeton: Princeton University Press, 1959), p.34
[13] Ibid, p.36.
[14] *The Space of Literature*, p. 256.
[15] Ibid, p.259.

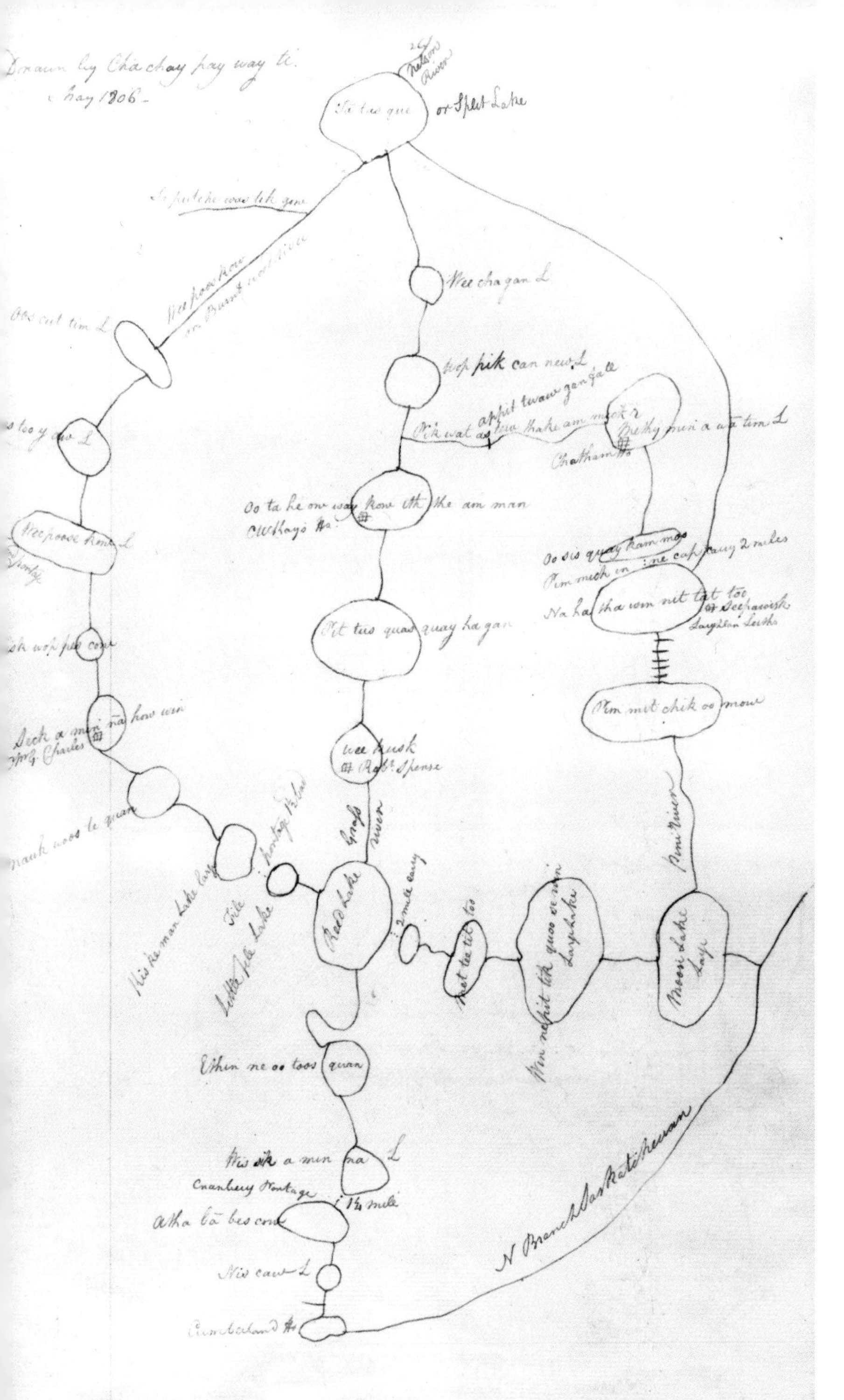

Sketch map of routes between Cumberland House and Split Lake 'Drawn by Cha chay pay way ti May 1806

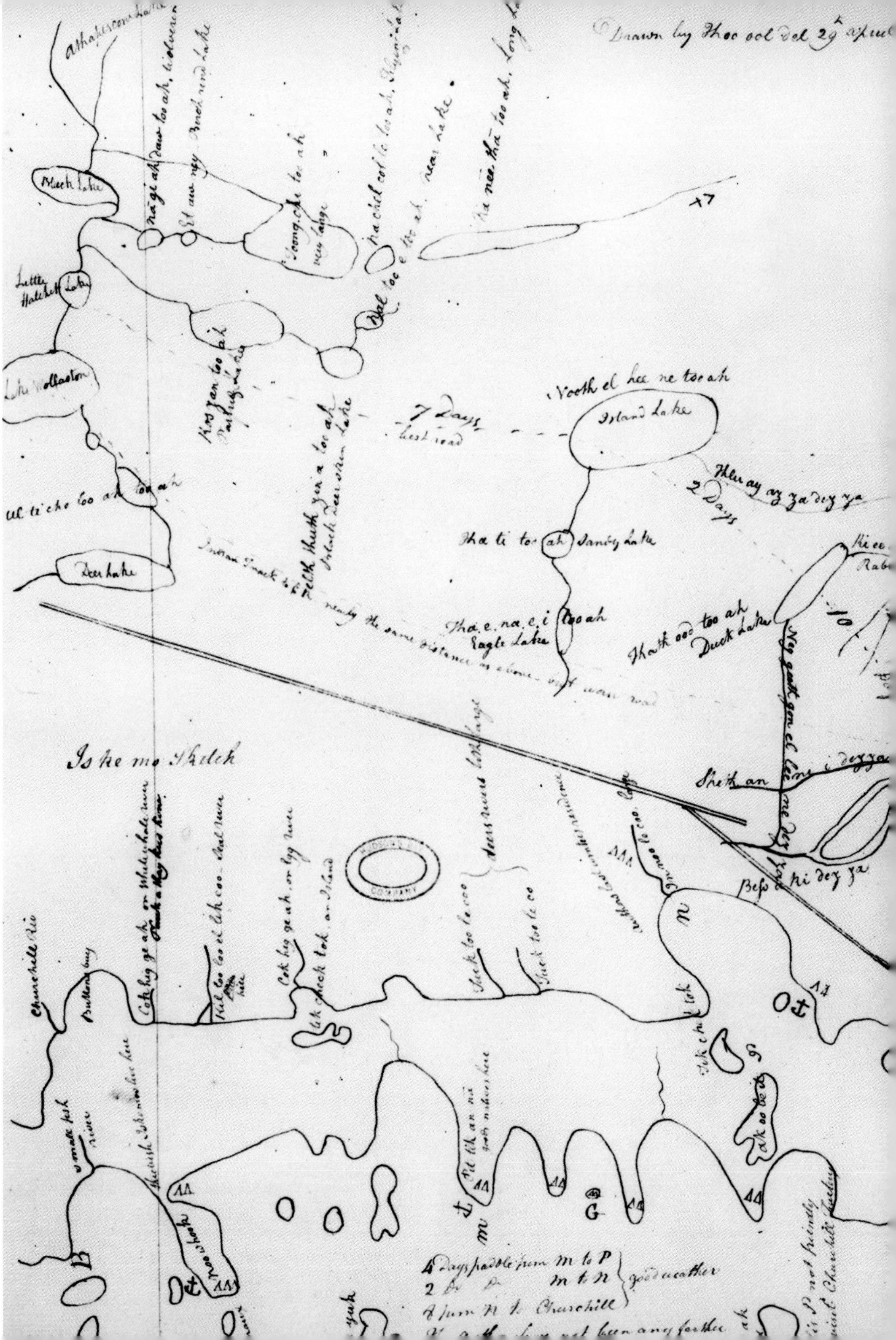

Drawn by Thoo ool del 29 april

Athapescow Lake

Black Lake

Little Hatchett Lake

Lake Wollaston

Deer Lake

Ul ti cho too ah too ah

Noo th el hee ne too ah

Island Lake

7 Days best road

2 Days

Tha ti too ah Sandy Lake

Tha e na e i too ah Eagle Lake

Thath ooo too ah Duck Lake

Indian Track to F. nearly the same distance as above but worse road

Is ke mo Sketch

Churchill Riv

Buttons bay

Deers rivers both large

Sheth an

M

Ot

G

B

4 Days paddle from M to P
2 Do Do M to N } good weather
8 from N to Churchill

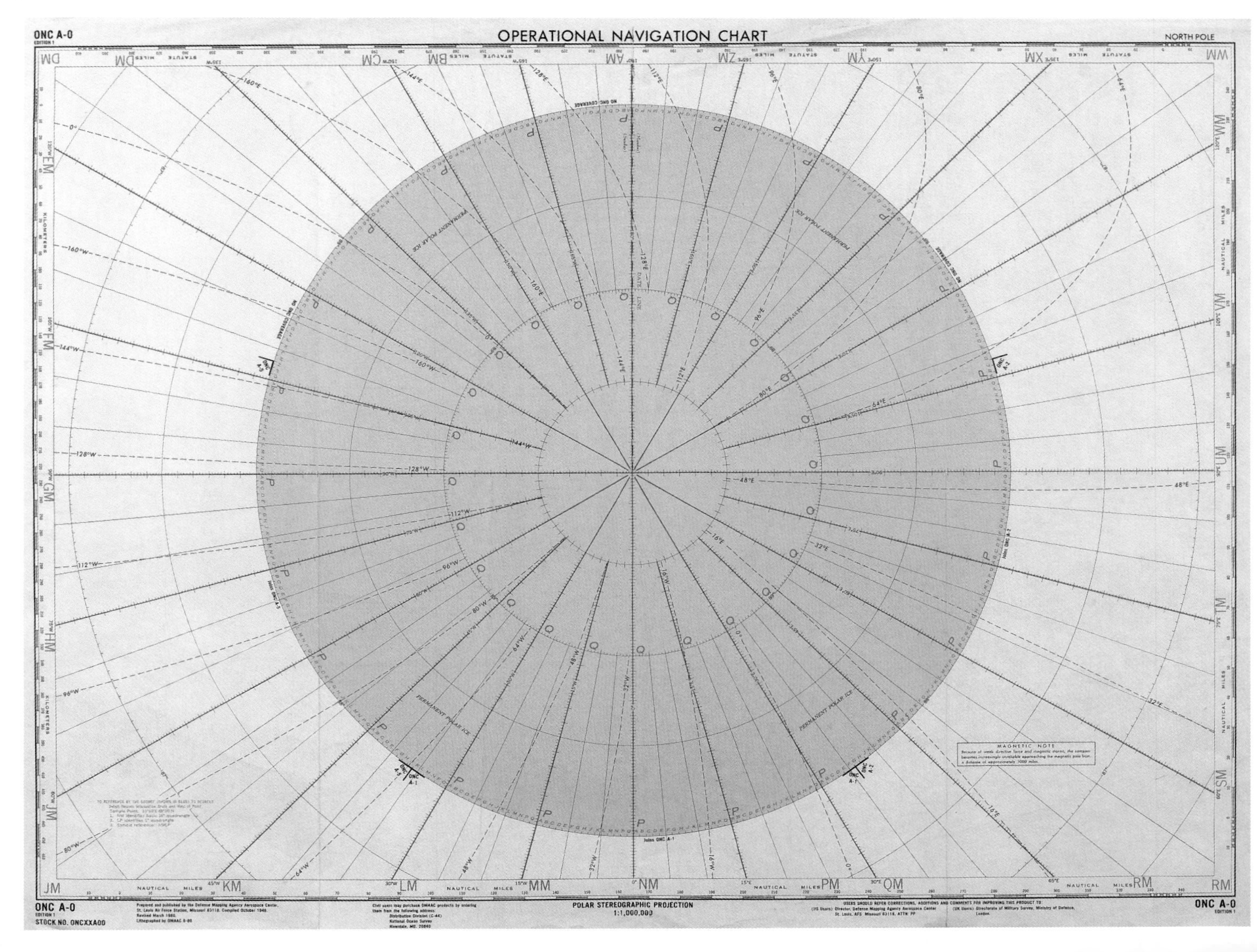

ONC A-0
EDITION 1
OPERATIONAL NAVIGATION CHART
NORTH POLE
PERMANENT POLAR ICE
NO ONC COVERAGE
DATE LINE
MAGNETIC NOTE
NAUTICAL MILES
STATUTE MILES
KILOMETERS
ONC A-0
EDITION 1
STOCK NO. ONCXXA0D
POLAR STEREOGRAPHIC PROJECTION
1:1,000,000
ONC A-0
EDITION 1

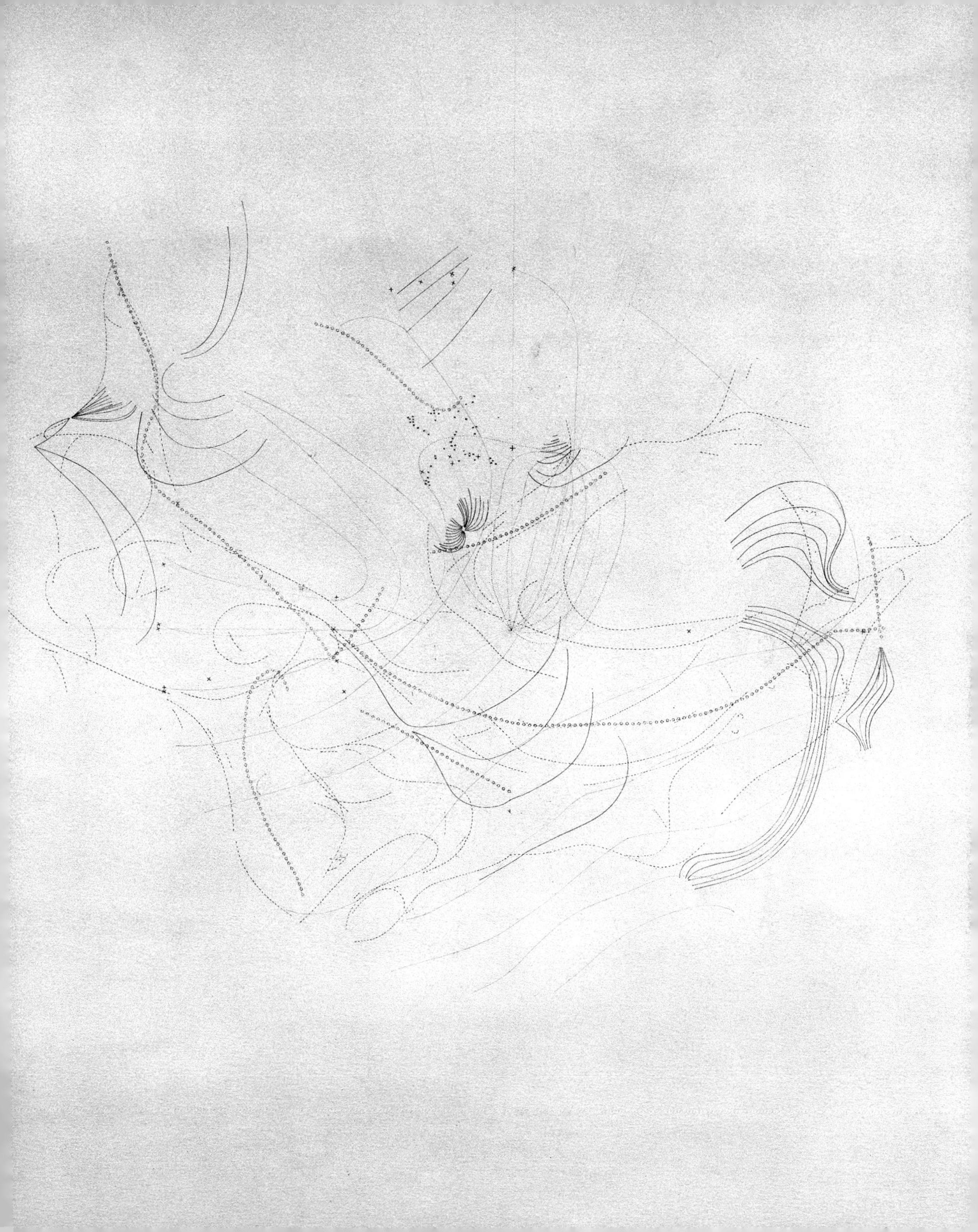

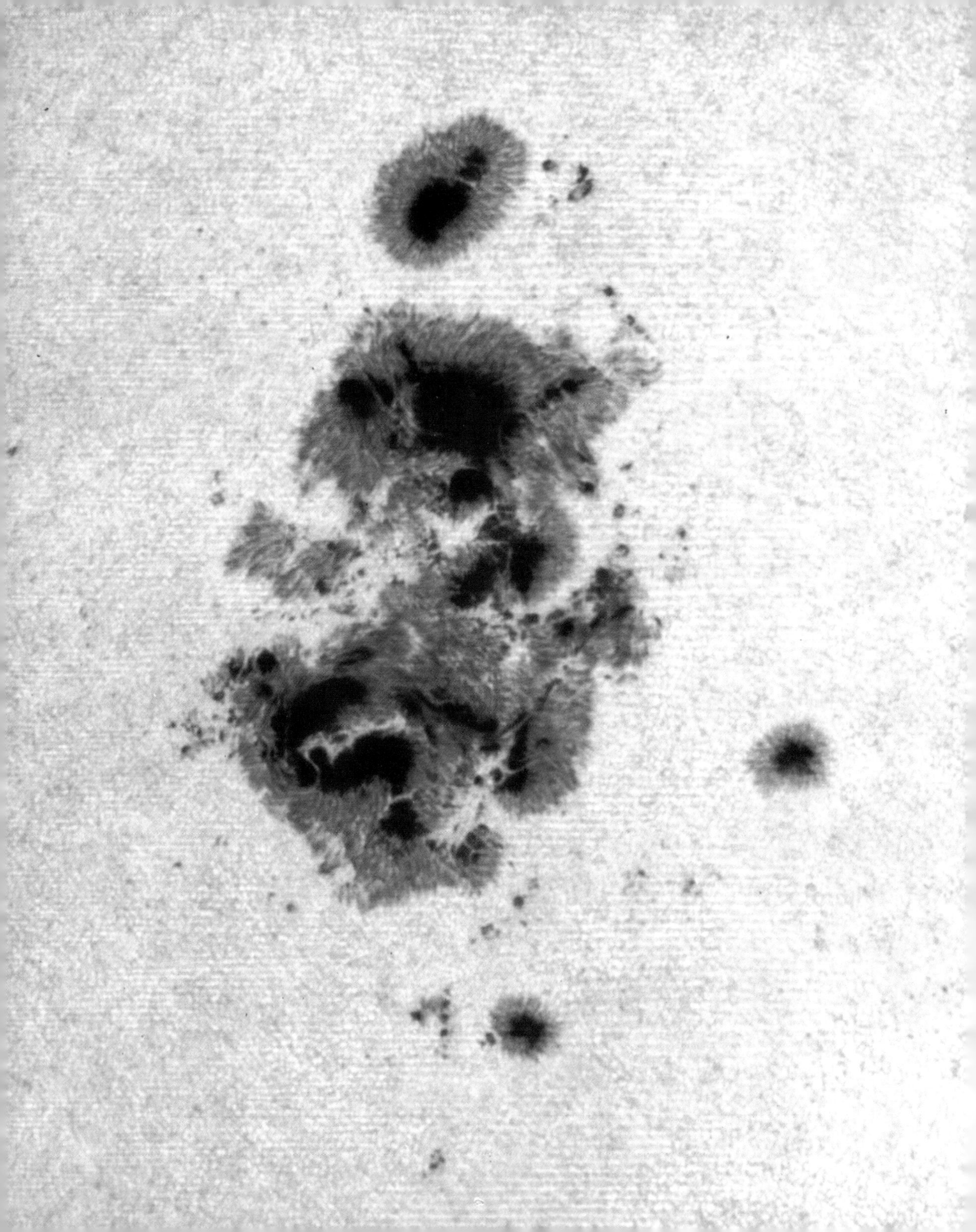

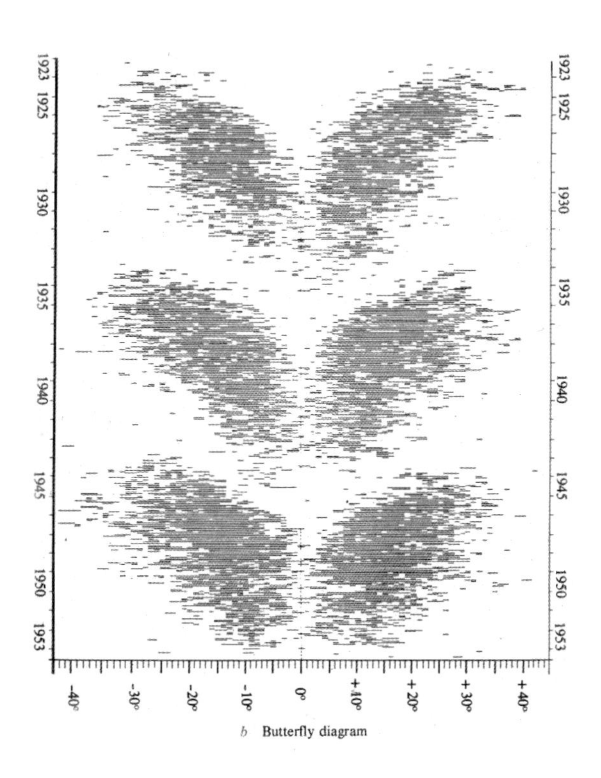

b Butterfly diagram

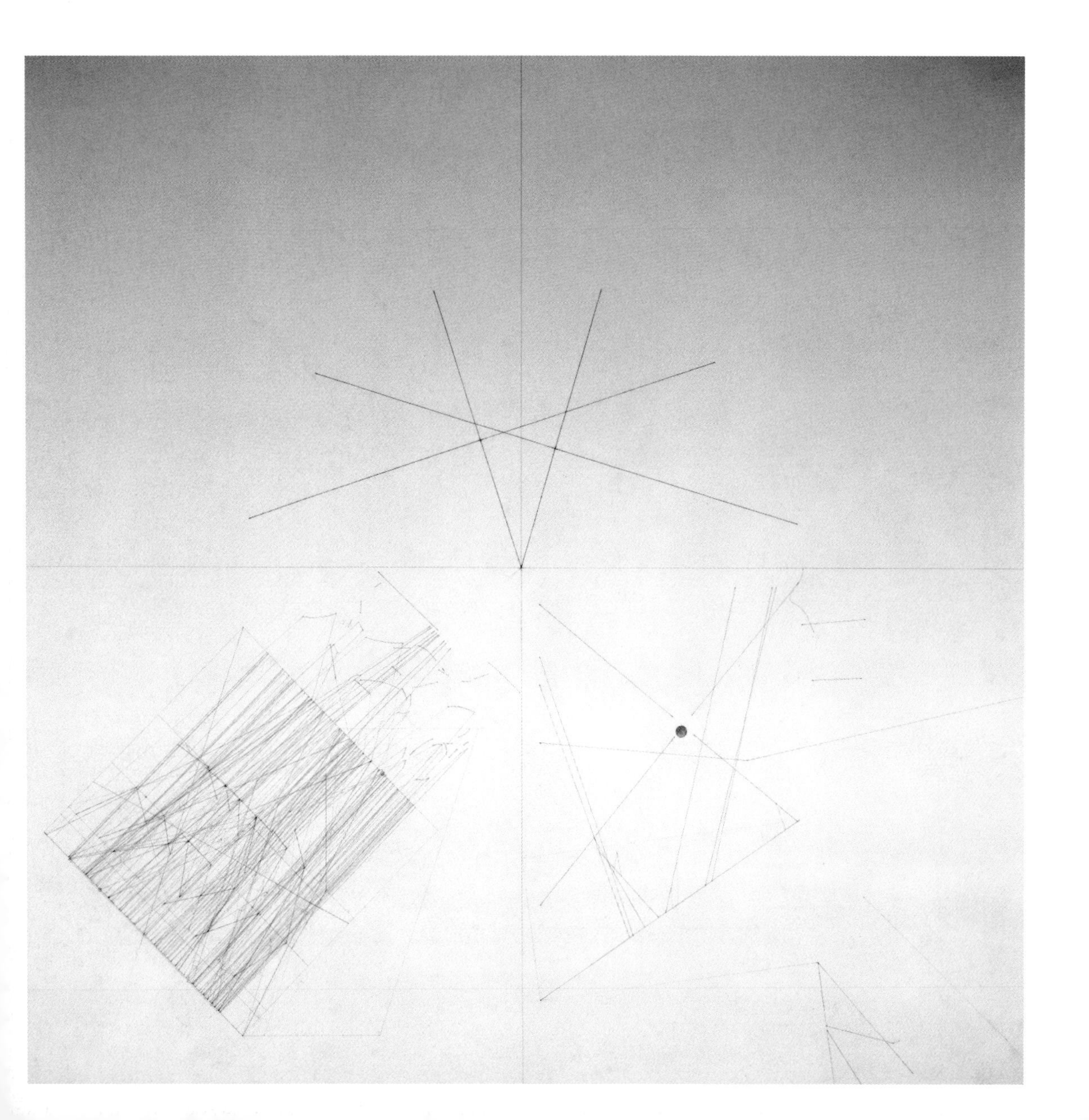

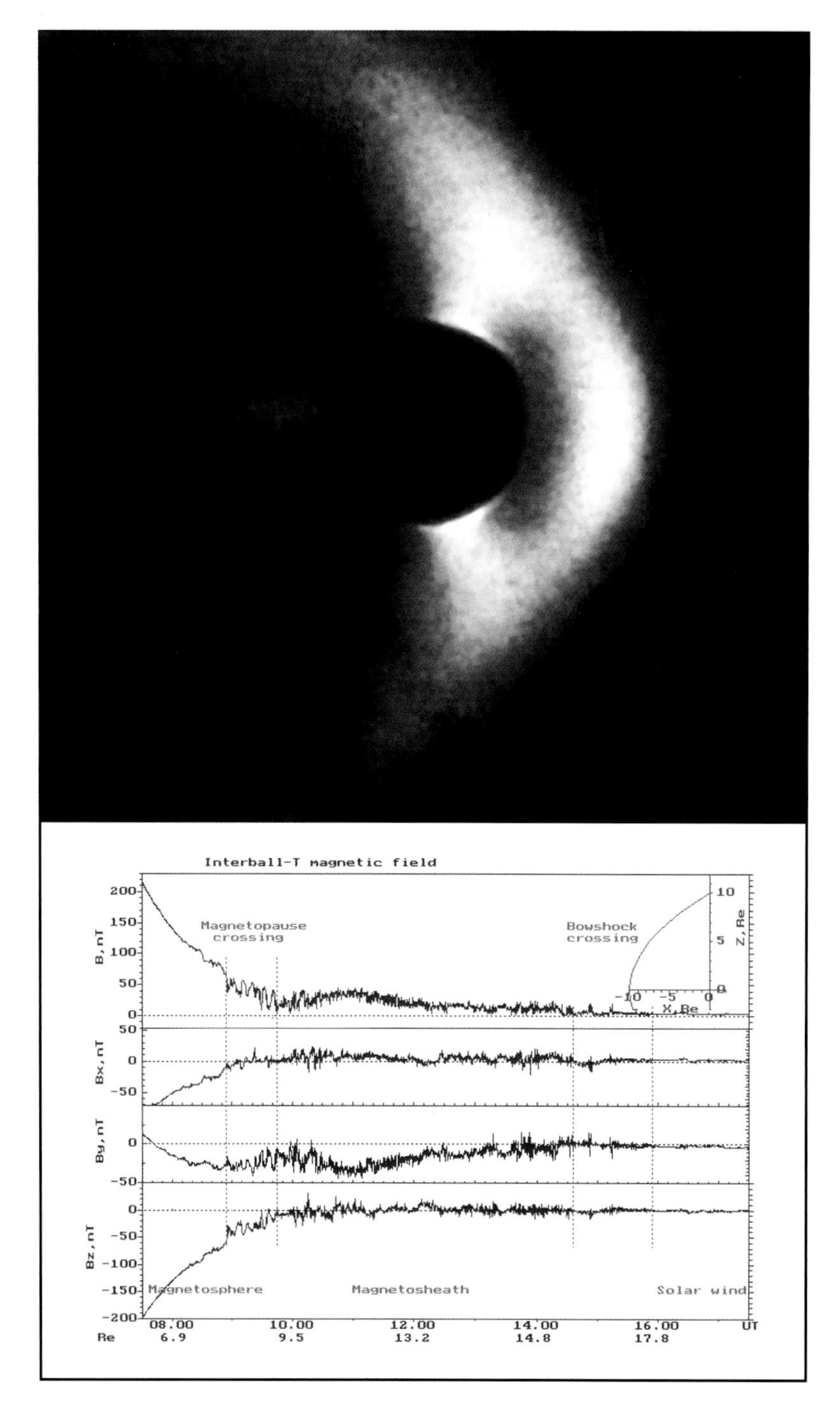

ELECTROMAGNETIC SPECTRUM

GAMMA	X-RAY	ULTRAVIOLET	VISIBLE	INFRARED	MICROWAVE	RADIOWAVE
$<10^{-10}$m	10^{-10}-10^{-9}m	10^{-9}-10^{-7}m	10^{-7}-10^{-6}m	10^{-6}-10^{-4}m	10^{-4}-10^{-1}m	$>10^{-1}$m

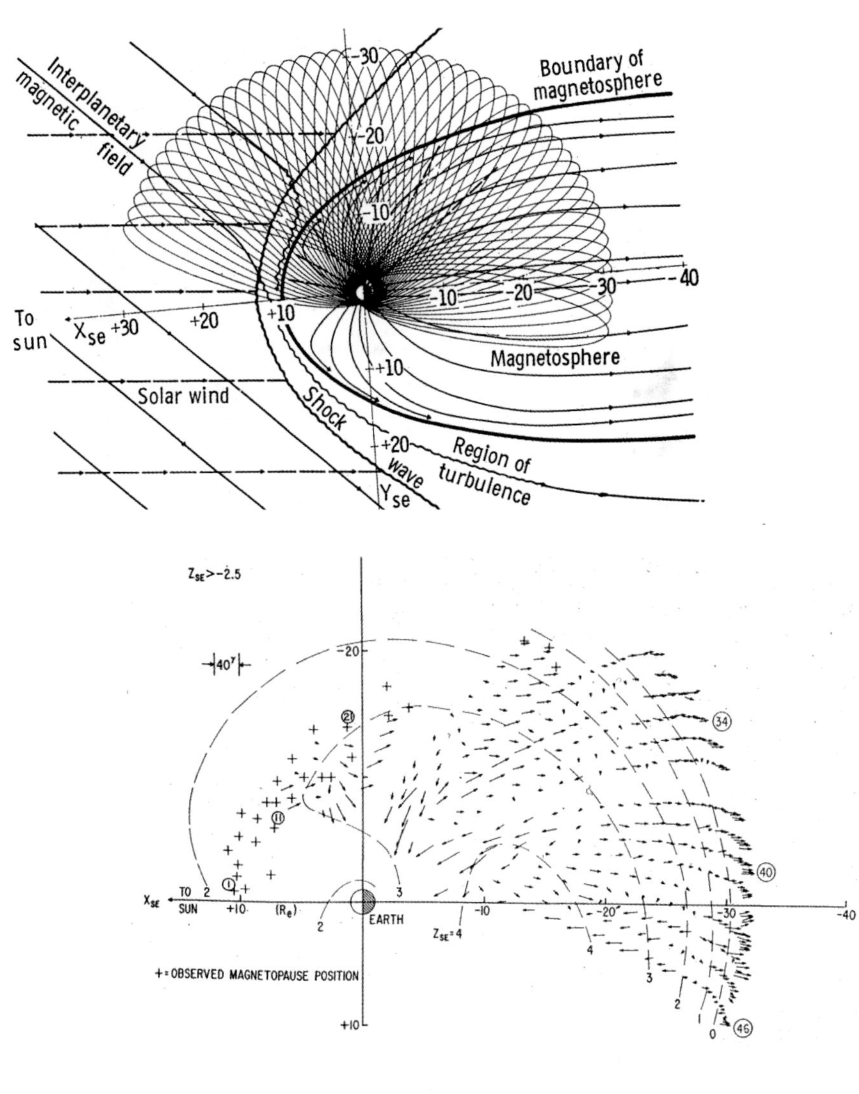

Interplanetary magnetic field
Boundary of magnetosphere
To sun
X_{se}
Magnetosphere
Solar wind
Shock wave
Region of turbulence
Y_{se}
$Z_{SE}>-2.5$
TO SUN
(R_e)
EARTH
$Z_{SE}=4$
+ = OBSERVED MAGNETOPAUSE POSITION

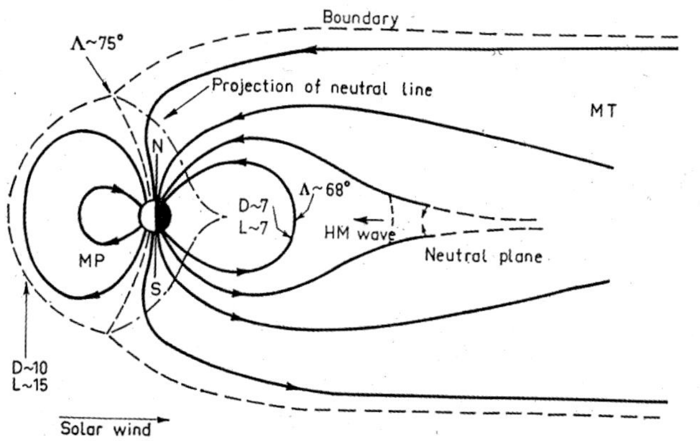

Boundary
Λ~75°
Projection of neutral line
MT
N
D~7
L~7
Λ~68°
HM wave
Neutral plane
MP
S
D~10
L~15
Solar wind

KEY

CEREMONY
Algonquin cosmology was shamanistic in structure. At the central axis of the universe was located a "great tree" which protruded into the "upper world." By climbing this tree, certain individuals, particularly shamans, could "reach very far up into the sky." The tree itself protrudes through a hole in the sky, an opening marked by the Pleiades, a circle composed of seven stars. In the initiation ceremonies of the shamanistic Midewiwen Society of the Ojibwa of the Great Lakes region, posts were erected in the microscopic Midewigan, the ceremonial structure, as surrogates for the World Tree of the Algonkian cosmos. In his definitive study of the Midewiwin, Walter Hoffman illustrates a birchbark scroll incised with images that served as mnemonic records of ceremonial procedure and sacred shamanistic songs. Among the numerous pictorial images employed, several Mide posts have been surmounted by birds, the most significant of which is the Owl, a bird often recurring in shamanistic ideology as the soul-bird, a vehicle of earthly transcendence for human souls. During the vision-quest undertaken at puberty by an Ojibwa youth, moreover, the fasting boy would sometimes perch like a bird in the branches of a tree, awaiting a vision from the spirits. The sacred tree or post of native American shamanism, however, is rarely rendered in two-dimensional pictorial form; it is visualized, instead, in structural and architectural terms as, for example, symbolic posts topped by feathers or an eagle's nest. [1]

Joan M. Vastokas

The Earth Will Know
A Woman Gave Birth to a creature of the twilight, all splotched and bristly—skinned, which no one could seem to identify. The angakok said: "The Earth will know." So they killed the creature and buried it in the ground, to learn what kind of thing it was. The ghost came back: a pretty little girl. [2]

Eskimo Point, Nunavut, Canada.

12 13 The landscape above the Arctic Circle is difficult to navigate because it always changes; it melts and freezes, icebergs migrate, fog obscures distance and sheets of ice cover the land and seal the waterways. The boundary between the land and the ocean are more or less undefined within the Arctic Circle. 1650.

14 15 These are some perceptions of the maps. The aerial photographs transform the maps into landscapes. The circle is the site for these drawings, and the draftsman revolves about the North Pole. This space exists in perceptual scale, between the drawing and the draftsman. These landscapes interrupt the white out and offer an exit strategy. The photographs draw hallucinations towards materiality.

16 A marvellous discovery was recently made, on August 13, 1856—The day which the first successful experiments took place. It was no less than direct supernatural writing by spirits without any intervening agency whatever—either a human medium, that is to say, or an inanimate object. [3]
August 13, 1856. 74 Rue de Chemin de Versailles, Paris.
Baron L. de Güldenstubbe

24 25 I have selected maps that were drawn by the First Nation people and later copied by the British surveyor, Peter Fidler. The maps limit a landscape that continuously changes; a solid line may shift or disappear as the landscape melts.
Peter Fidler surveyed the territories in and around Rupert's Land for the Hudson Bay Company during the 18th and 19th centuries. He mapped the frontier as he moved through it, drawing what he saw through a perceived scale. Sometimes he measured distance with time.

24 Sketch map of routes between Cumberland House and Split Lake 'Drawn by Cha chay pay way ti May 1806. In Peter Fidler's Journal of Exploration.

25 Sketch maps Drawn by Thoo ool del 29th April 1809' of routes from 'Athepescow Lake' to 'Sea Coast' (top). Iskemo sketch coastlines from Churchill to Chesterfield Inlet 'Drawn by Nay hek til lok an Iskemo 40 years of age, 8th July 1809 (lower). Redrawn by Peter Fidler. Distance is measured with time.

The program is scale.

26 Aerial photograph of map 3—landscape.

27 Aerial photographs of map 5—landscapes.

28 29 Aerial photograph of map 5—landscape.

30 Operational Navigation Chart. Polar Stereographic Projection, the origin of the circle is the North Pole.

31 Map 1, Log. Measured boundaries of phenomena. Positive and Negative Ionization belts, Magnetic Anomalies, Magnetic Declination, Ocean Currents, Ice Sheets.

32 A large sunspot group photographed on May 17,th1957. The effects of solar magnetism are visible in the sunspot. Sunspot activity causes great magnetic storms on earth.
Although it is true that heat energy flows only from hot to cold (by thermal conduction or radiation), other forms of energy appear in the solar surface that do not have such a restriction...Two such forms of energy underlie the two most obvious surface features on the Sun. One of these features is sunspots, dark vortices where strong magnetic fields stop the outward flow of heat energy and thus cause the surface to cool and become dark. The other feature is granulation, the seething convective eddies of rising and descending turbulent motions in the outer layers of the Sun. Each feature is proof of the importance of a different type of energy: sunspots reveal magnetic energy strong enough to halt convective energy flow; the granulation reveals the kinetic energy of its turbulent motions. Either magnetic or kinetic energy can propagate from one place to another with little regard to which is hotter. [4]

33 The butterfly diagram represents the repeating sunspot phenomenon within chronological time, demonstrating an 11 year cycle.
The phase of the sunspot cycle also determines the mean heliographic latitude of all groups. At a minimum the first groups of the new cycle appear at ± 30°—35°. Thereafter the latitude range moves progressively towards the equator, until by the next minimum the mean latitude is around ± 7°. Then, while the equatorial groups are petering out, those of the succeeding cycle begin to appear in their characteristic higher latitudes. This latitudinal progression is known as Sporers law. At any one time there may be a considerable spread in latitude, but groups are seldom seen farther than 35° or closer than 5° from the equator. The butterfly diagram is a graphical representation of Sporers law obtained by plotting the mean heliographic latitude of individual groups of sunspots against time...The strength of this field is further enhanced by the pertrubing effect of convection, which twists the field lines into rope-like configurations that may penetrate through the surface to form sunspots. This will occur first in intermediate latitudes, where the rate of shearing of the field is greatest, and thereafter in increasingly low altitudes. [5]

34 Map 2—The North Pole, Magnetic North Pole, Geomagnetic North Pole, Ocean currents. Magnetic Declination Tableau: Arctic Circle, 70°—80°N.
Memory retrieval—theta brainwave frequency: 4—7 Hertz (cycles per second).

35 Map 3—Magnetic Anomalies over three instants of time. The sphere is projected onto a plane. This chart is a construction document. Map 3—p. 64.

36 Map 2—detail: Magnetic Declination Chart.

37 Map 5—detail: vertical ice sheet. Horizontal threshold between liquid and vapour, ice forms at the edges.

Paris,1859. From the evening of August 28th until the morning of the 29th the needles of the magnetic telegraph at Paris were almost constantly in motion, as if a permanent current was passing through the telegraph wires. Business was therefore entirely interrupted and could not be resumed until 11 a.m. Aug. 29th. The same effect was noticed on the telegraph lines from 4h to 8h on the morning of Sept. 2, although no aurora was noticed on that day. Business was again interrupted, the needles were disturbed, and the bells were rung. [6]

38 The chart represents the effects of terrestrial magnetism on the solar wind entering the magnetosphere.

39 The magnetosphere shields the planet from most of the oncoming solar radiation. It is surrounded by the magnetopause where ionized particles are directed by the earth's magnetic field, followed by a shockwave that encloses the turbulent magnetic field. The outer belt (10,000—65,000 km above the earth's surface) is mainly composed of electrons and the inner belt (650—6300 km) of protons.

Quebec, 1989.
A great magnetic storm occurred on 13 March 1989, that caused a nine-hour blackout of the 21,000 MW Hydro Quebec electric power system. A vivid description of that failure has been provided by G. Blais and P. Metsa (1993) of Hydro Quebec: "Telluric currents induced by the storm created harmonic voltages and currents of considerable intensity on the La Grande network. Voltage asymmetry on the 735-kV network reach-

ed 15%. Within less than a minute, the seven La Grande network static var compensators on line tripped one after the other...With the loss of the last static var compensator, voltage dropped so drastically on the La Grande network (0.2 p.u.) that all five lines to Montreal tripped through loss of synchronism (virtual fault), and the entire network separated. The loss of 9, 450 MW of generation provoked a very rapid drop in frequency at load-centre substations. Automatic underfrequency load-shedding controls functioned properly, but they are not designed for recovery from a generation loss equivalent to about half system load. The rest of the grid collapsed piece by piece in 25 seconds. [7]

45 Data Field. Encasement. Lines of magnetic anomalies cut through a solid. This is a construction document.

46 Map 3—field detail.

47 Map 3—field detail through coordinate.

48 49 Caught points. 0,0 field.

50 51 Map 4—details. Map 4—p. 68.

52 Map 5—detail: horizon: 60°. The data begins to solidify. Map 5—p. 84.

53 Map 2—relationship of magnetic declination to the ocean currents below, a pulse. Location: Arctic Ocean, Svalbard.

We read in the records of animal magnetism, of a blind lady, who, in her sleep, admirably described the beauties of nature. Having recovered her sight, she owned that nature, during sleep, was much more beautiful than she found it on awaking. [8]

54 Map 3—detail of vertical plane.

55 Map 3—detail of 0,0 line. Location: Arctic Ocean, Greenland Basin/ International Date Line.

56 Construction Site between 70°N and 80°N. Geomagnetic Reference Field: North—South component (X), East—West component (Y), Vertical component (Z), Inclination (degrees), Declination (degrees).

57 The solid blocks. Construction document.

58 59 Construction.

60 61 Map 4—detail of 0°, 90°E.

62 63 Map 4—detail of 180°W, 90°W.

64 Map 3. Magnetic anomalies over three instants of time, between 70°N—80°N. The sphere is compressed into a plane.

65 Map 3—detail of an anomaly through a coordinate. Construction detail.

66 67 Map 3—detail.

68 Map 4—Material translation of data at 0°, 90°E, 180°, 90°W. After cutting the data into the 10°x10° wood blocks, the residual geometries are recorded. The North Pole is located in the centre of the map.

69 Map 5—Landscape. Horizon: 112°.

70 71 Data field. A stream of electromagnetic anomalies form 0°, 90°E, 180°, 90°W transferred to wood. The solid blocks. Construction document.

74 75 Map 5—detail, 0,0 datum, cut ocean current.

76 The construction is made with magnetic anomaly data. The data are cut into solid blocks within an envelope of 10° longitude x10° latitude. They begin at the earth's surface and extend into the magnetosphere. North is up. The construction site is between 70°N and 80°N. The remaining solids compose the construction.

77 The cuts.

78 79 Construction: maps 2,3,4: 170°E, 180°E, 170°W, 10°W, 0°, 10°E, 80°E, 90°E, 90°W, 80°W.

A poor woman in very feeble health, complained in the dispensary at Stratford, that she constantly saw faces and figures cut in half. Sometimes these apparitions appeared in a crowd, resembling a number of heads eagerly looking in at the door or window.
Patients of a third class are governed by the images that harass them; they cannot give their attention to the sensations which proceed from objects that are present; they continue to talk to persons whom they imagine near to them, and do not recognize the voices of their friends; their eyes are turned towards them, but they have apparently assumed other forms and faces; they look around the room, and think themselves in a strange place. In this state, it is impossible for them to compare the true sensations, which they are incapable of receiving, with the false ones which they alone recognize. They cannot compare what they see with what, in their febrile condition, they have forgotten, and the necessary consequence of this defect is delirium or active insanity. [9]

84 Map 5—Four bodies float on the surface of the water reorienting the geometries that encase them. Liquid/Solid/Vapour. Location: cut ocean current.

85 Map 6—A construction of scale through a stair in a photographed space between 180° and 170°W. The drawing's scale is 1:50.

86 87 Map 6—detail.

88 89 Map 5—detail. Ice planes along the cut ocean current.

90 Map 3—detail.

92 93 Aerial photograph of map 5—landscape.

94 95 Construction of map 5 and map 6: 4 encasements for 4 bodies. An evacuation of space through a point.
The construction is translated with a photograph of the first construction. The photograph limits and frames the cuts and a scale is found in this space. In this case, scale is constructed through a stair, figured out in map 6, in which the space of the photograph collapses into a point—the pupil of a body standing on the stair. There are four bodies on this stair and each body is encased in a solid.

96 97 Map 6—detail, scale, stair, the foot.

98 99 Aerial photographs of map 5—landscapes.

102 103 Solar Solstice Envelope. 6'x6' body grid.

1 Joan M. Vastokas, "The Shamanic Tree of Life," *Arts Canada*, (December 1973/ January 1974), 140.
2 Millman, Lawrence, *A Kayak Full of Ghosts* (Northampton, Mass: Interlink Books, 2004), p. 69.
3 Grillot de Givry, *Witchcraft, Magic and Alchemy* (New York: Dover, 1971), p. 173,174.
4 Robert W. Noyes, "A Matter of Degrees," in *Revealing the Universe*, ed. James Cornell and Alan P. Lightman (Cambridge Mass: MIT Press, 1982), p.91.
5 "Sunspot Cycle," *A Dictionary of Astronomy*, 1979, 327.
6 *Effect on the telegraph wires.* Comptes Rendus T.XLIX.
http://www.spaceweather.gc.ca:80/historyeffects_e.shtml. (29 Mar. 2005)
7 Blais G. and Metsa P., *Operating the Hydro-Québec grid under magnetic storm conditions since the storm of March 13, 1989*, Proc. Solar-Terrestrial Predictions Workshop, Ottawa, May 18-22, 1992, ed. J. Hruska, M.A. Shea, D.F. Smart, G. Heckman, vol 1, 108-130, 1993.
http://www.spaceweather.gc.ca:80/historyeffects_e.shtml. (29 Mar. 2005)
8 Brierre De Boismont, *Hallucinations: The Rational History of Apparitions, Visions, Dreams, Ecstasy, Magnetism and Somnabulism* (Philadelphia: Lindsay and Blakiston, 1853), p.258.
9 Ibid, 266.

MAGNETIC DECLINATION CHART

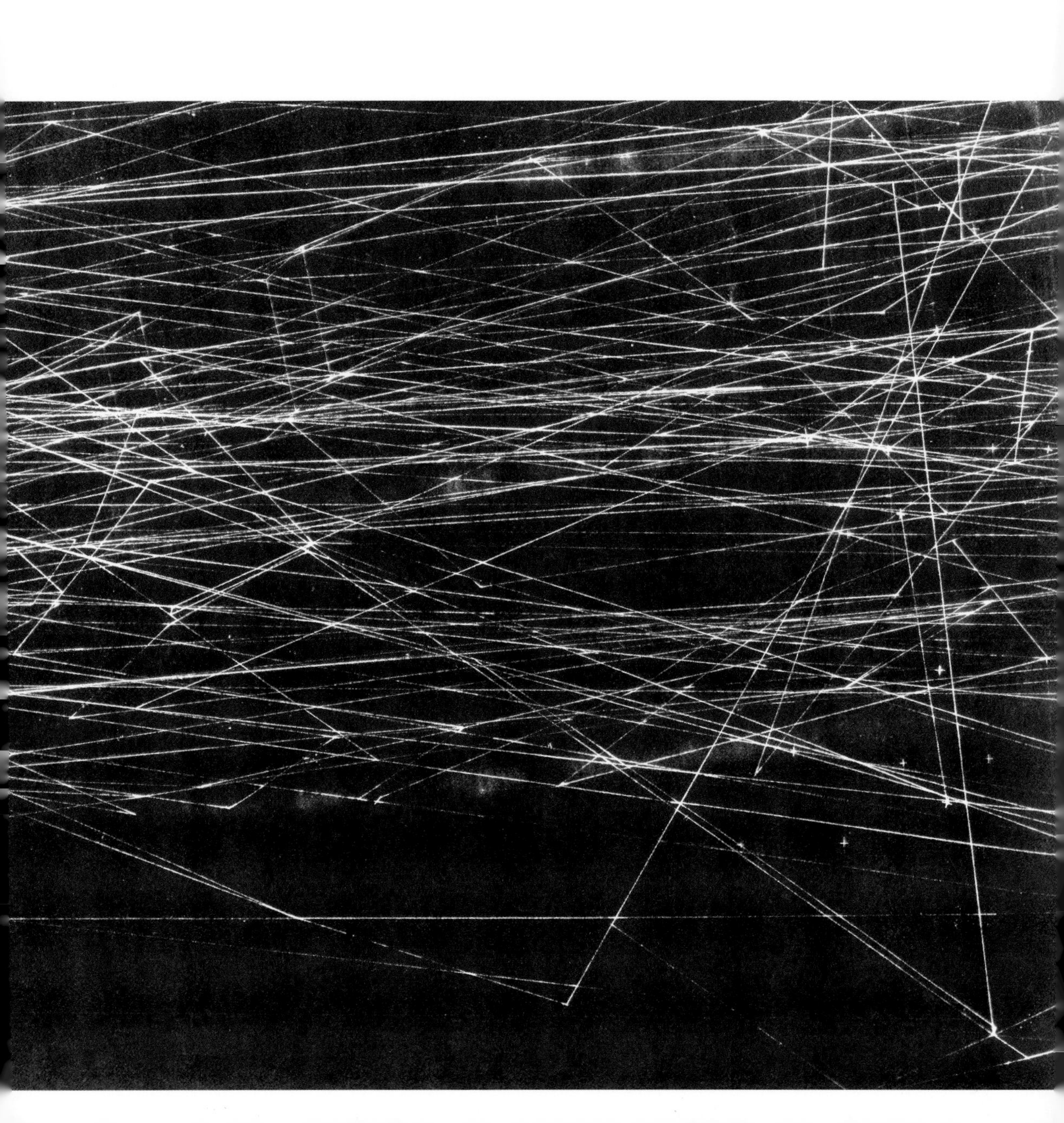

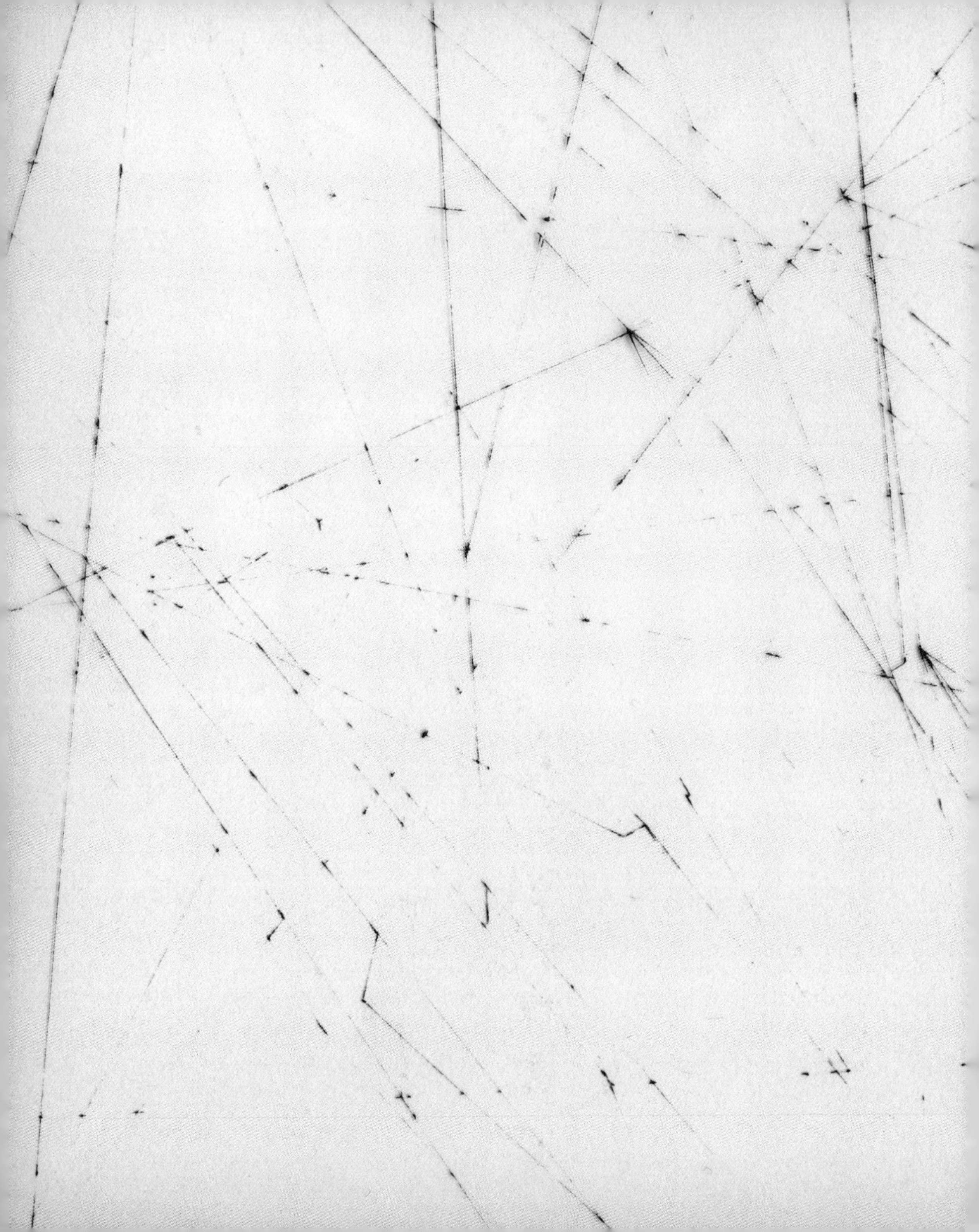

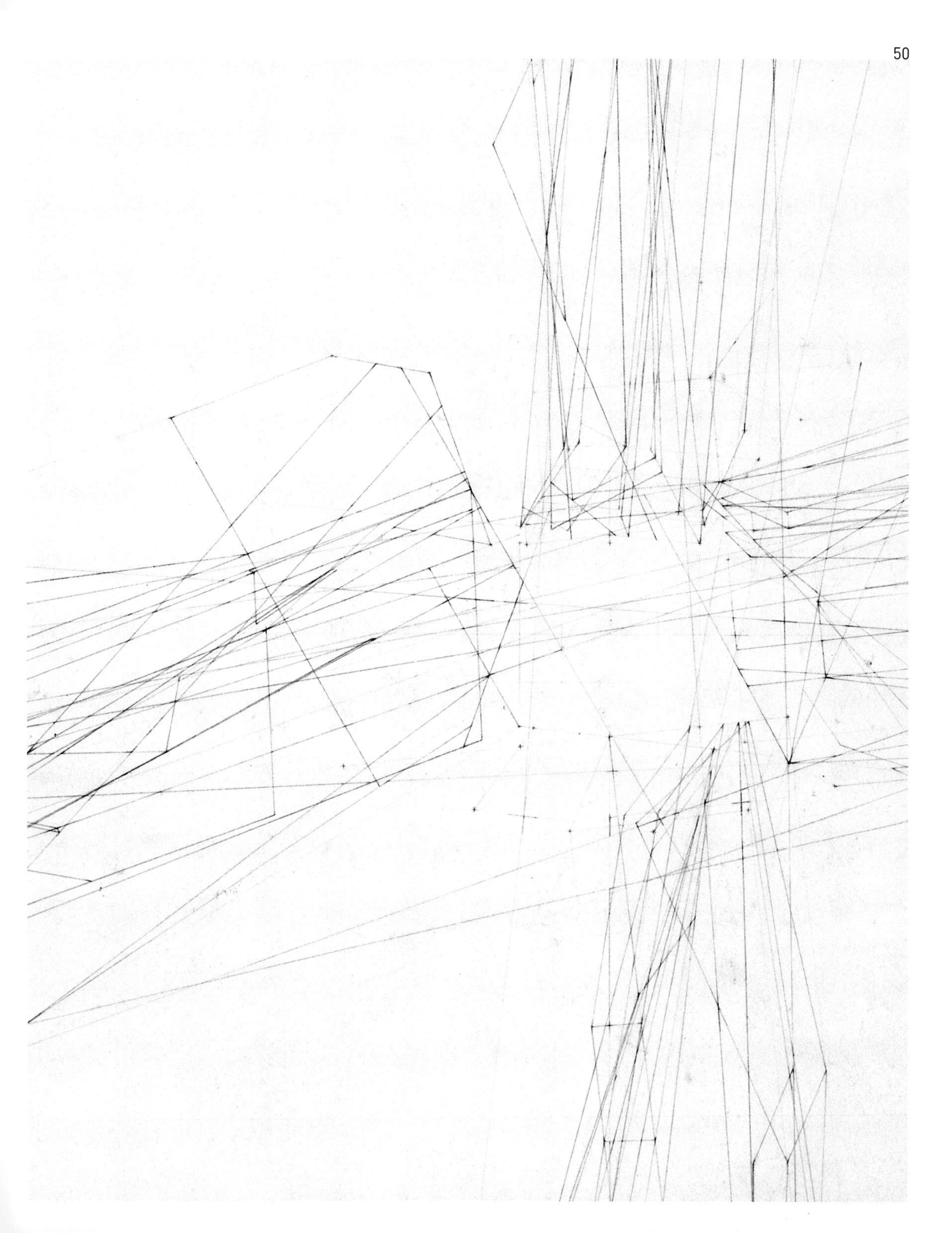

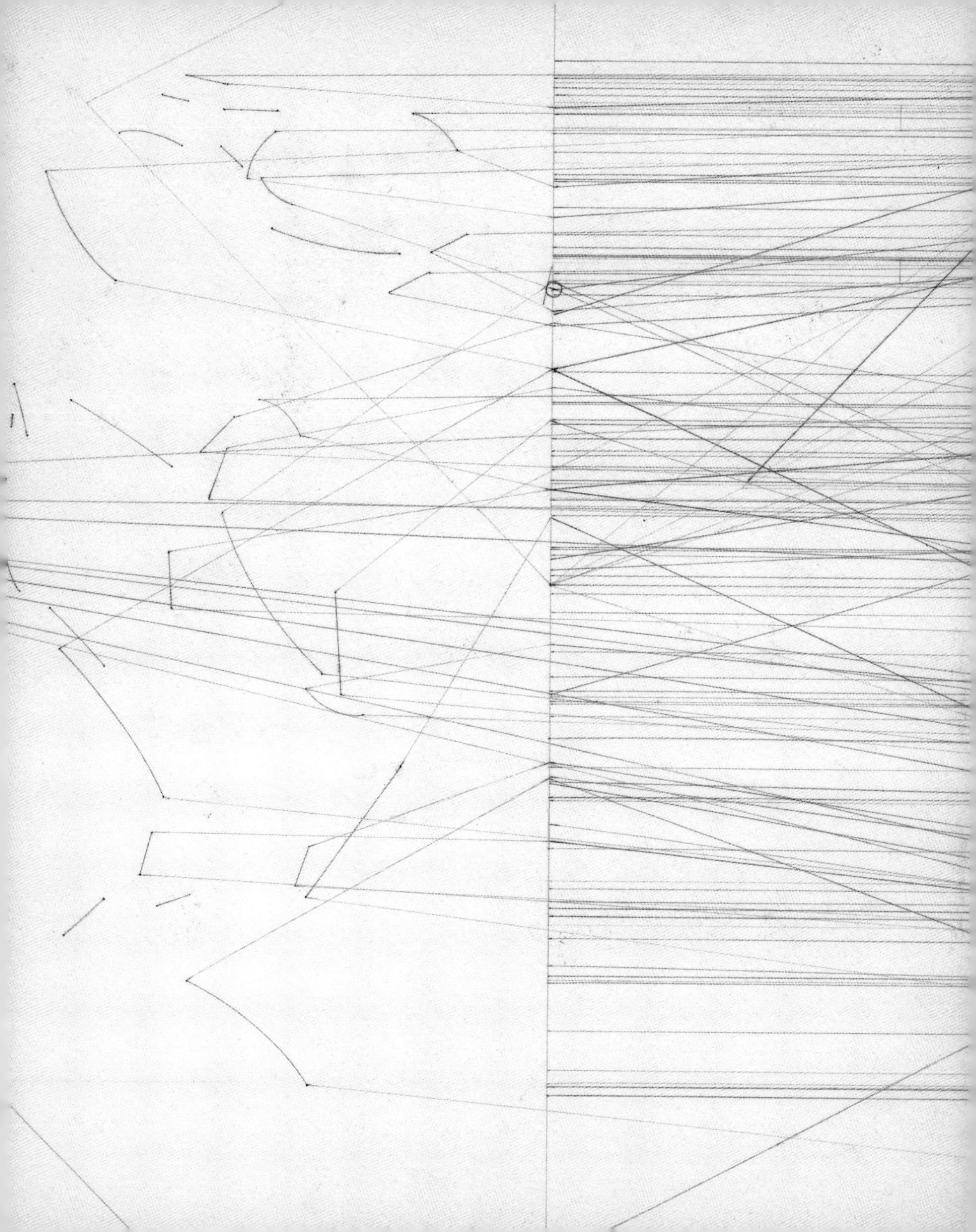

Construction site: 70°N—80°N

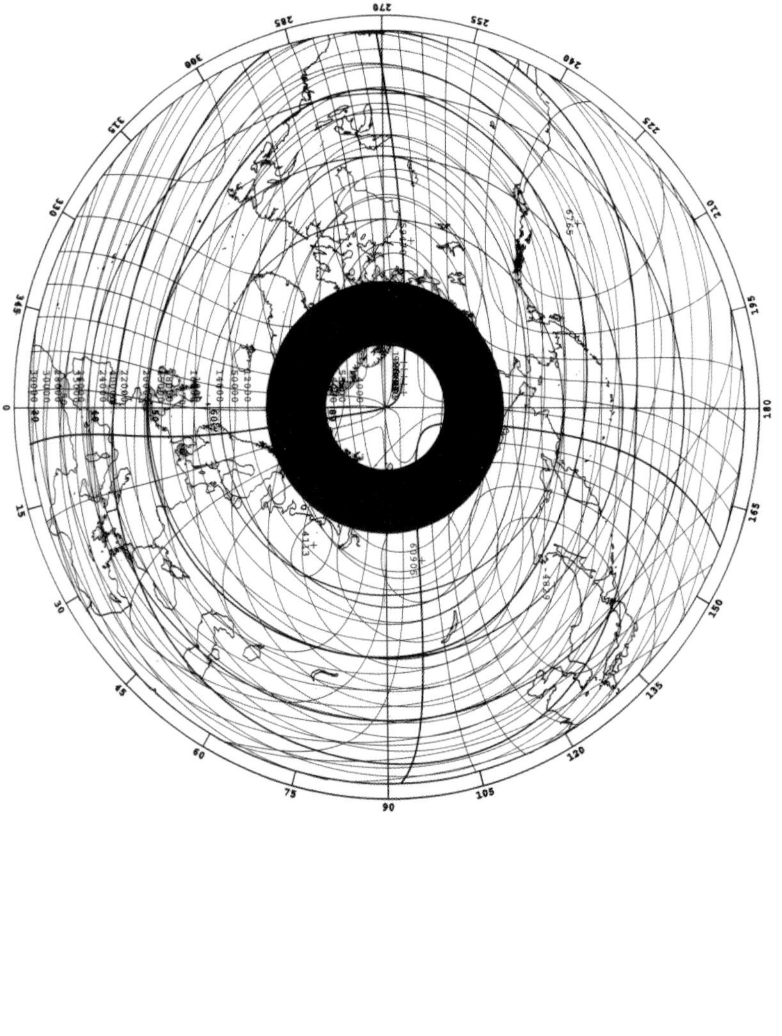

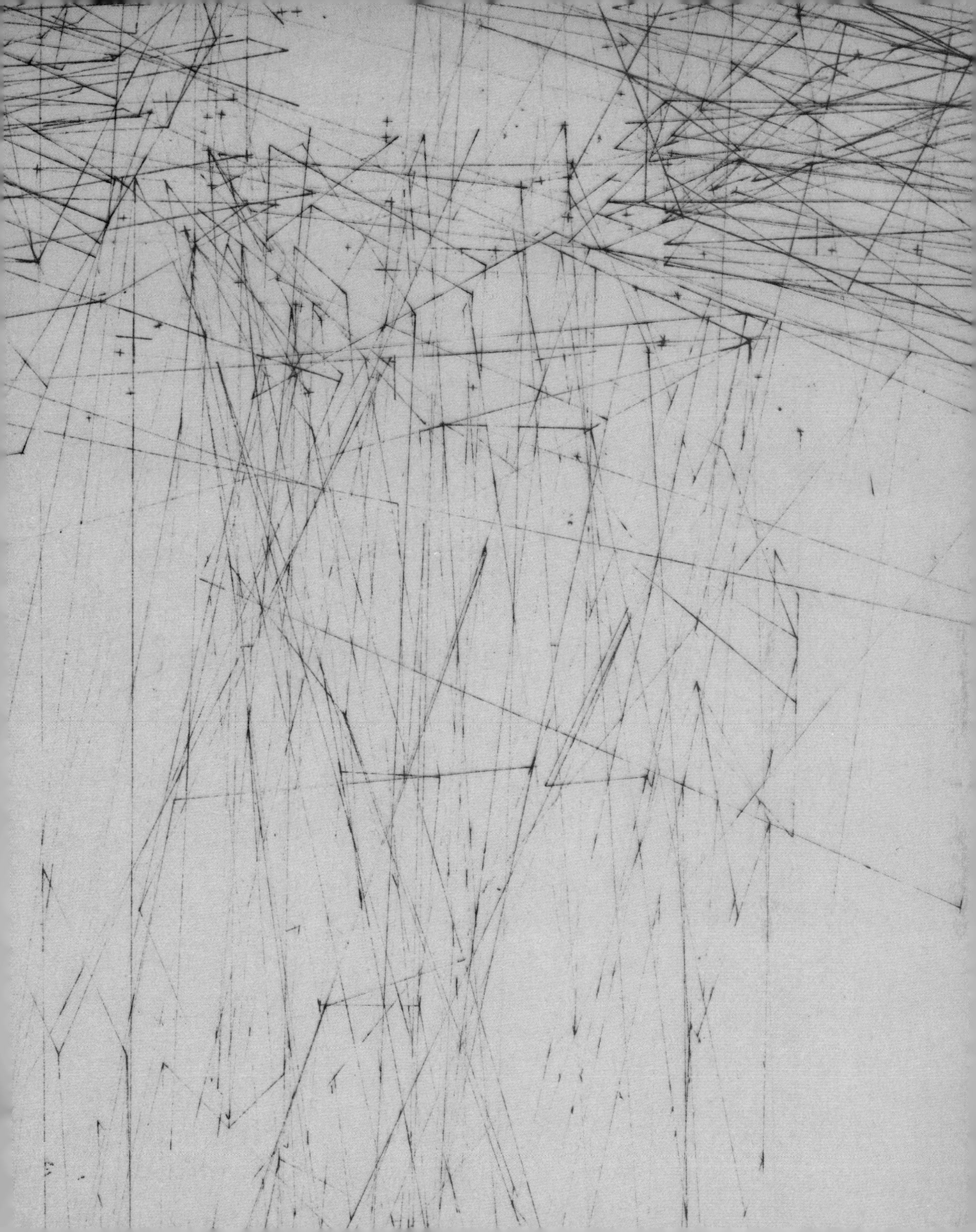

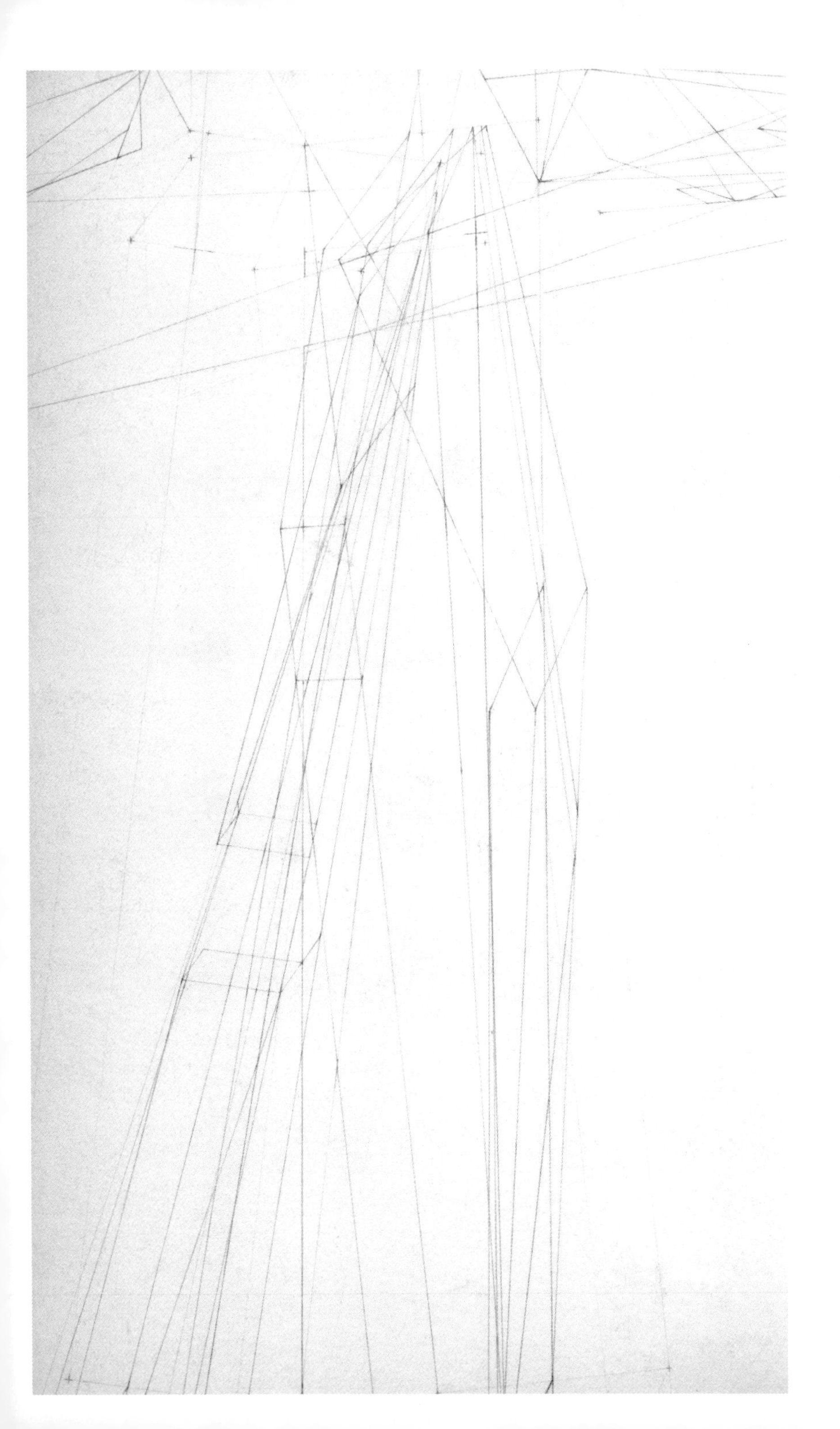

0°

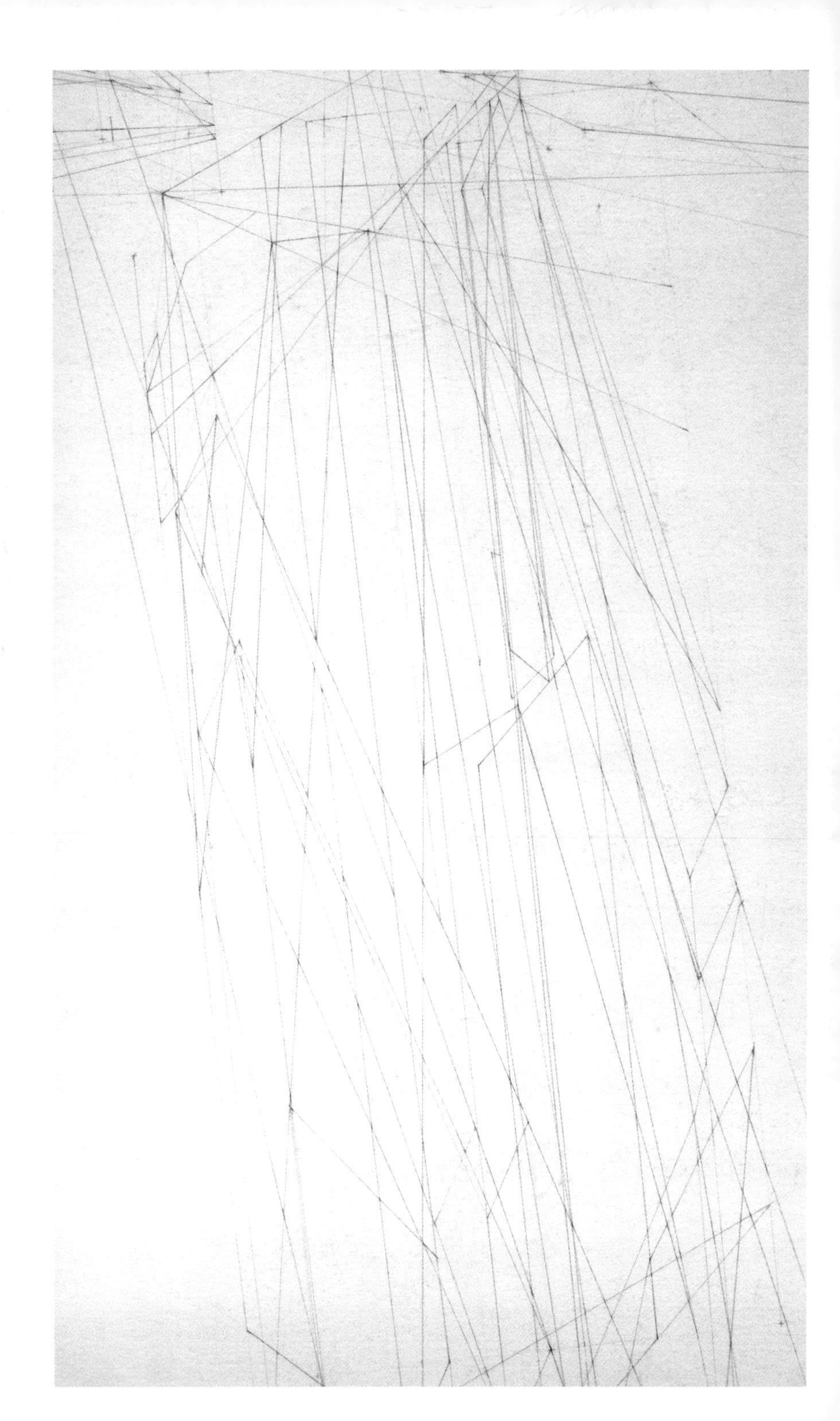

90° E

180°

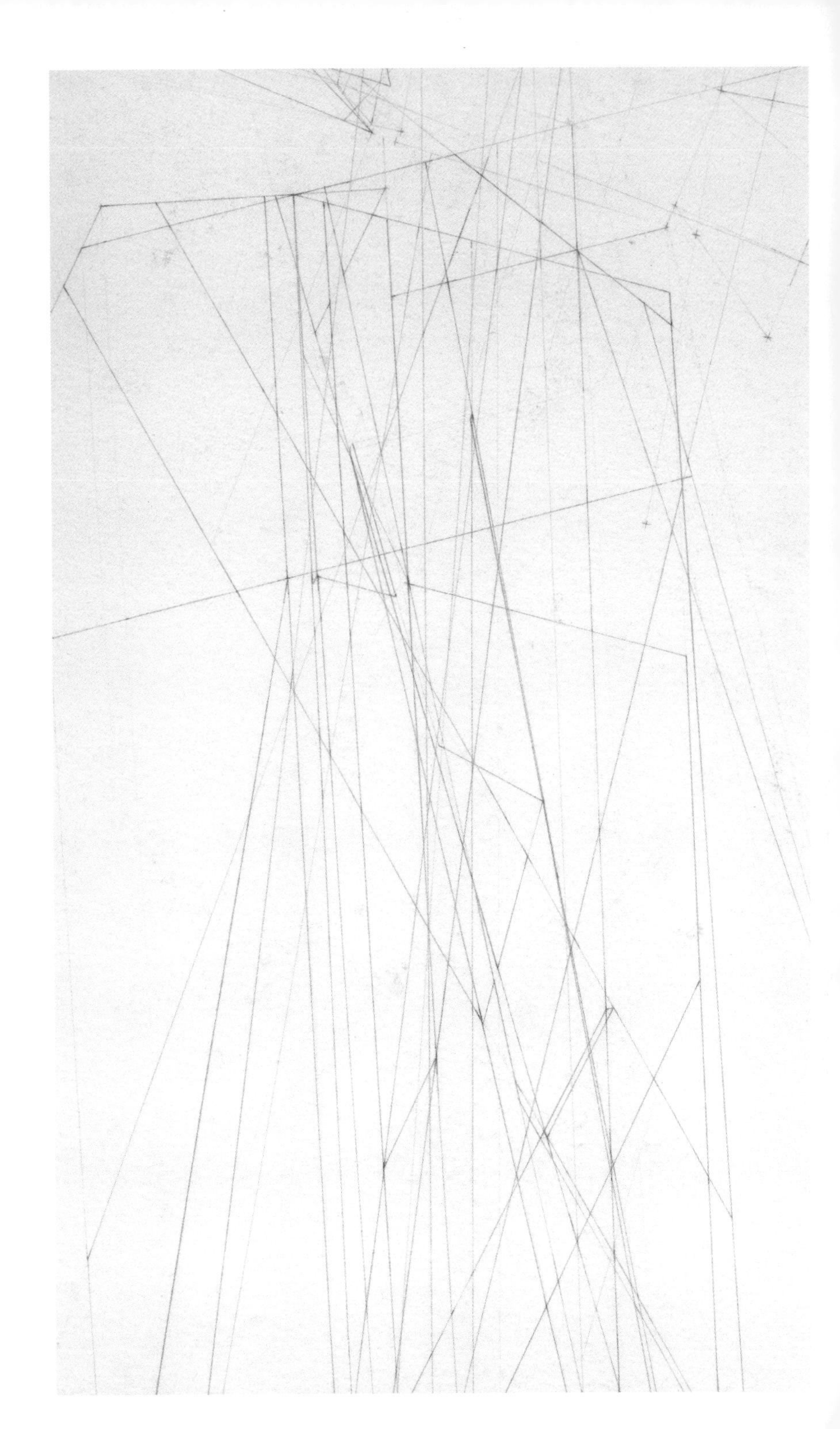

90° W

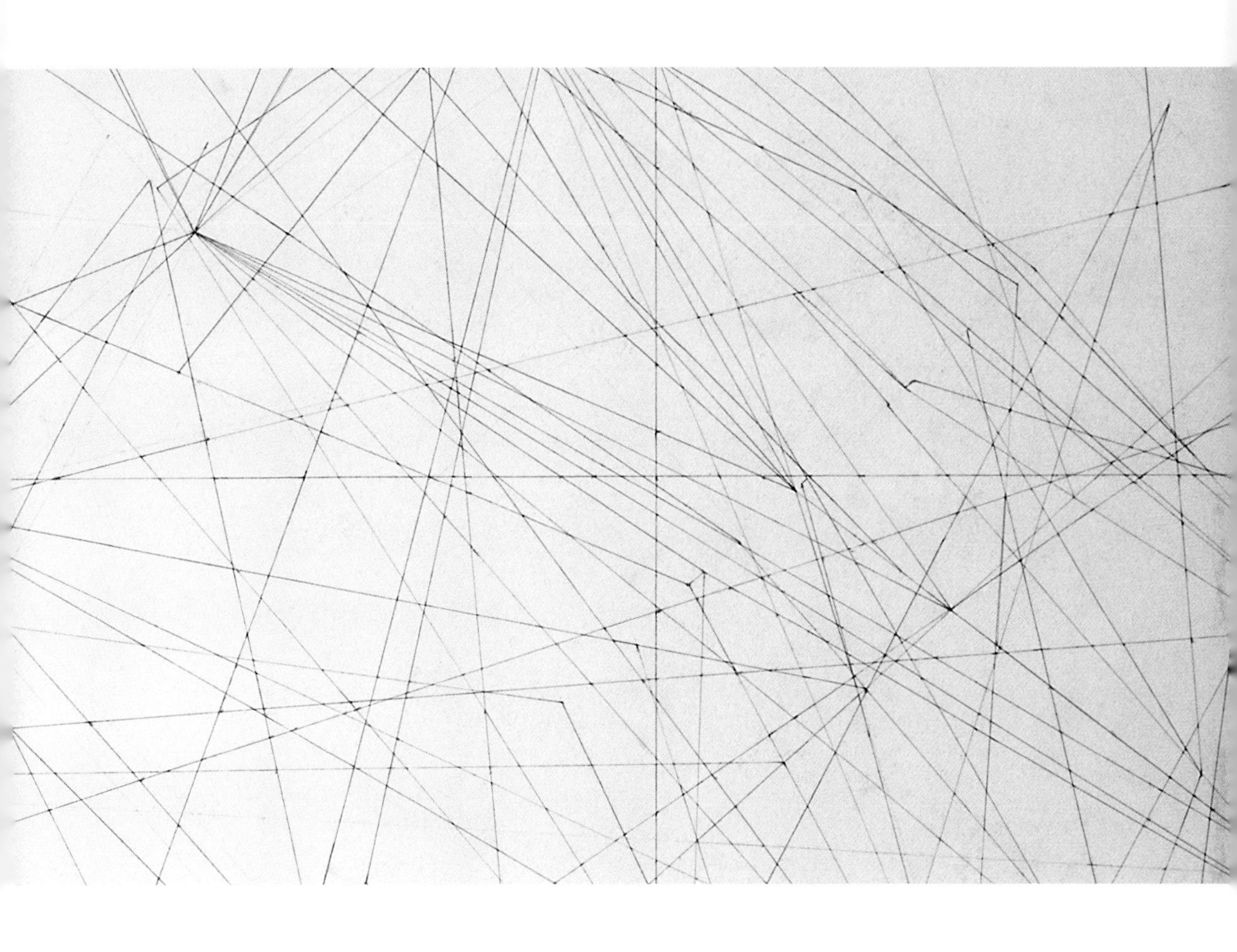

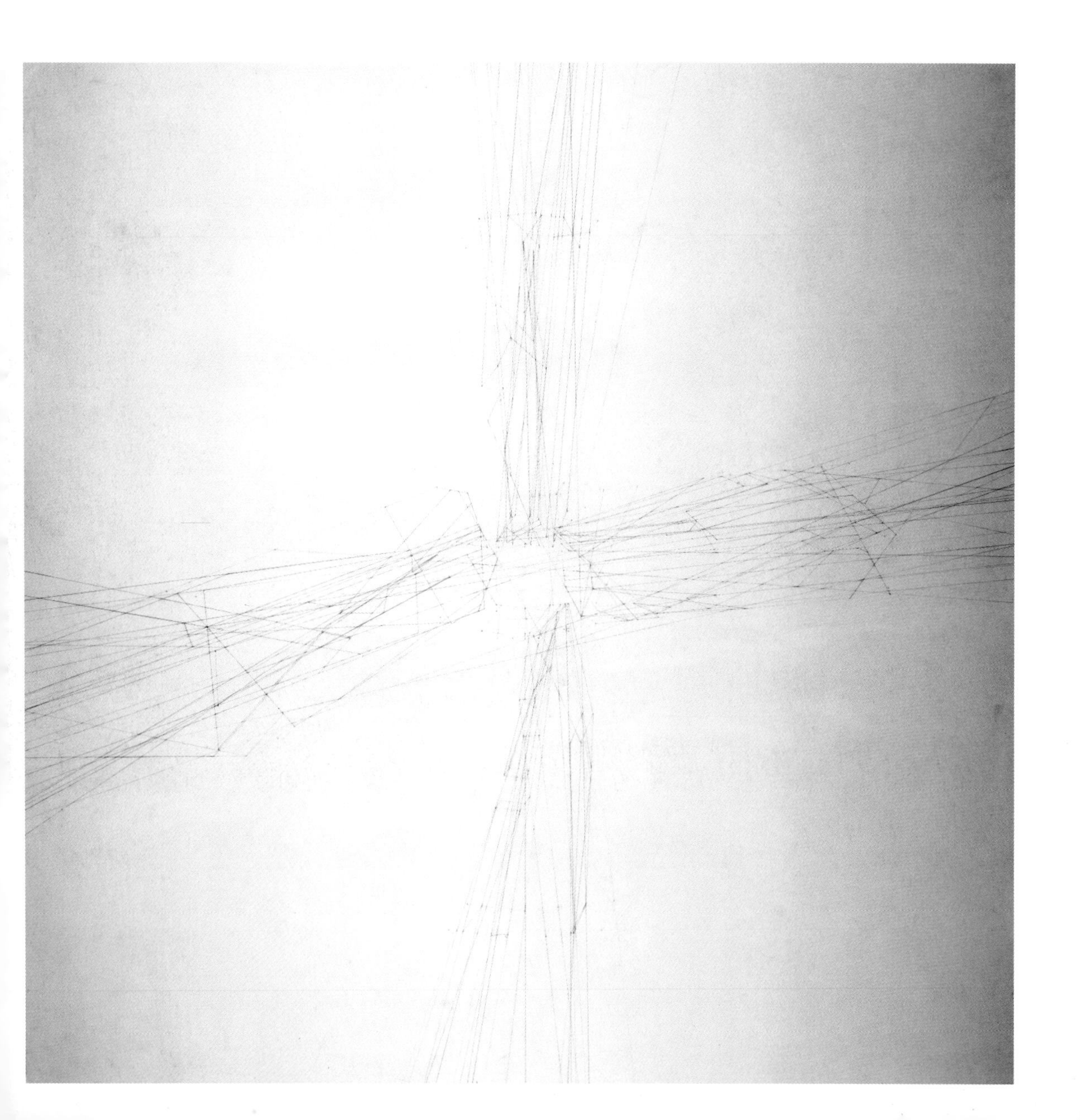

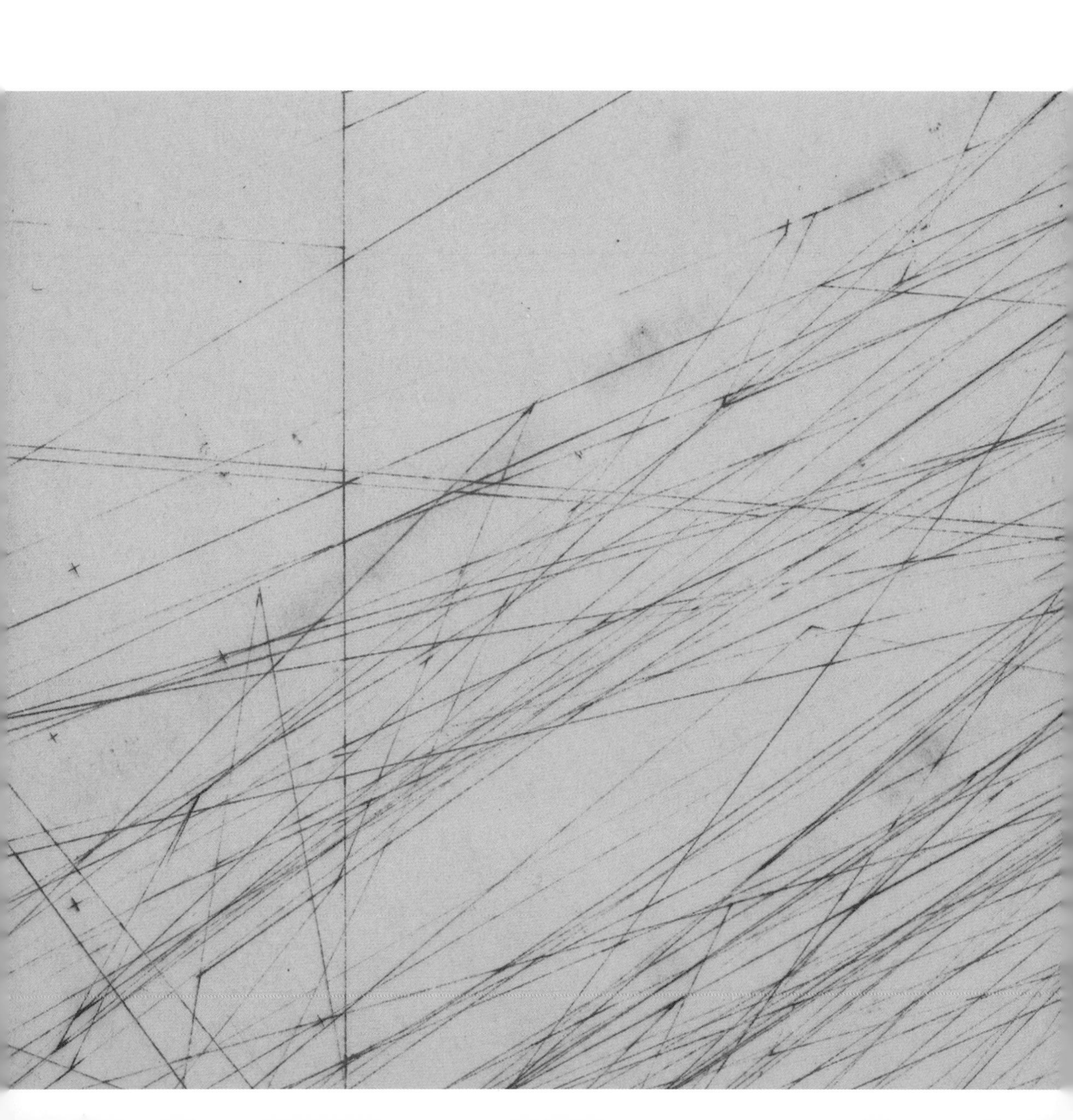

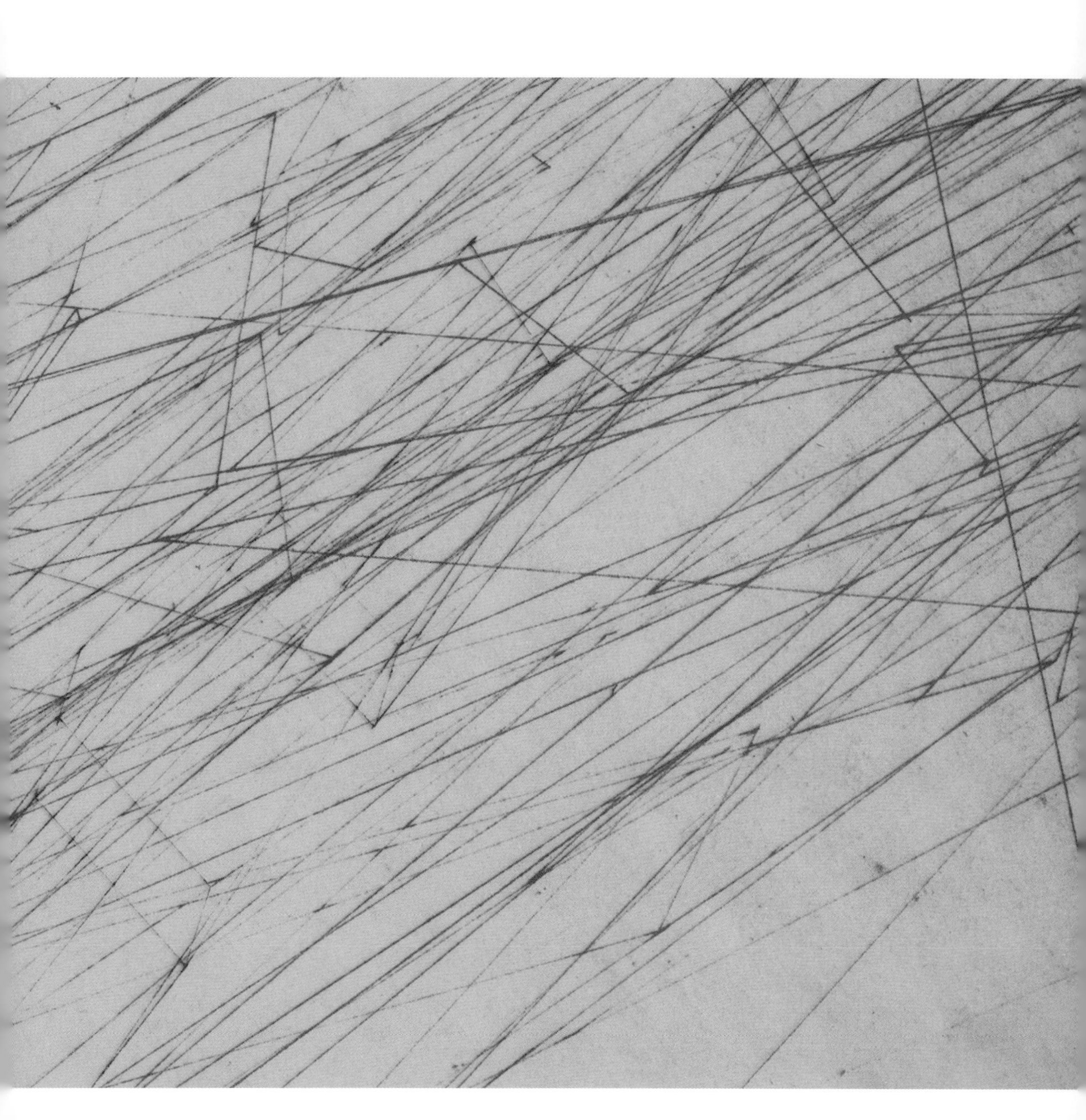

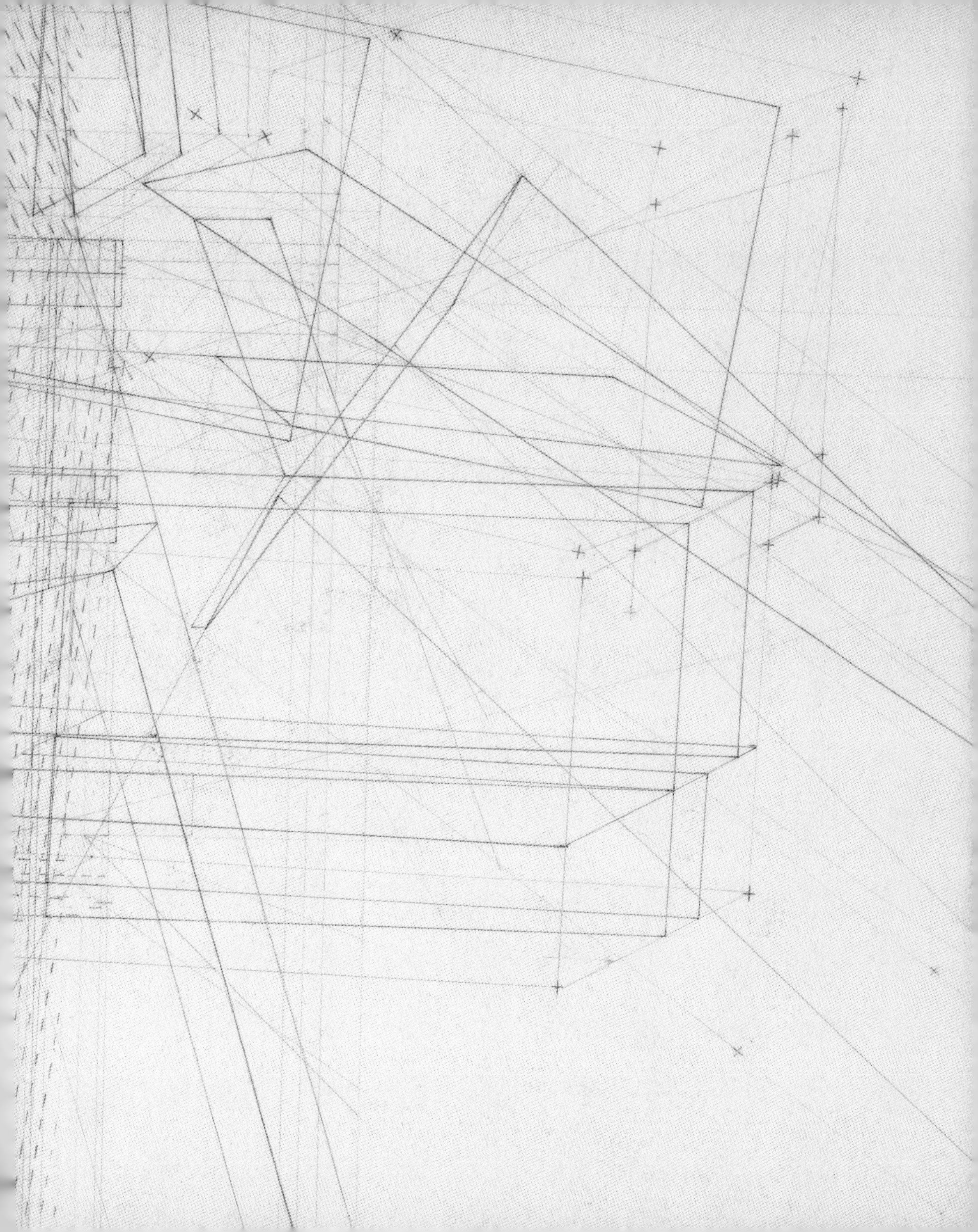

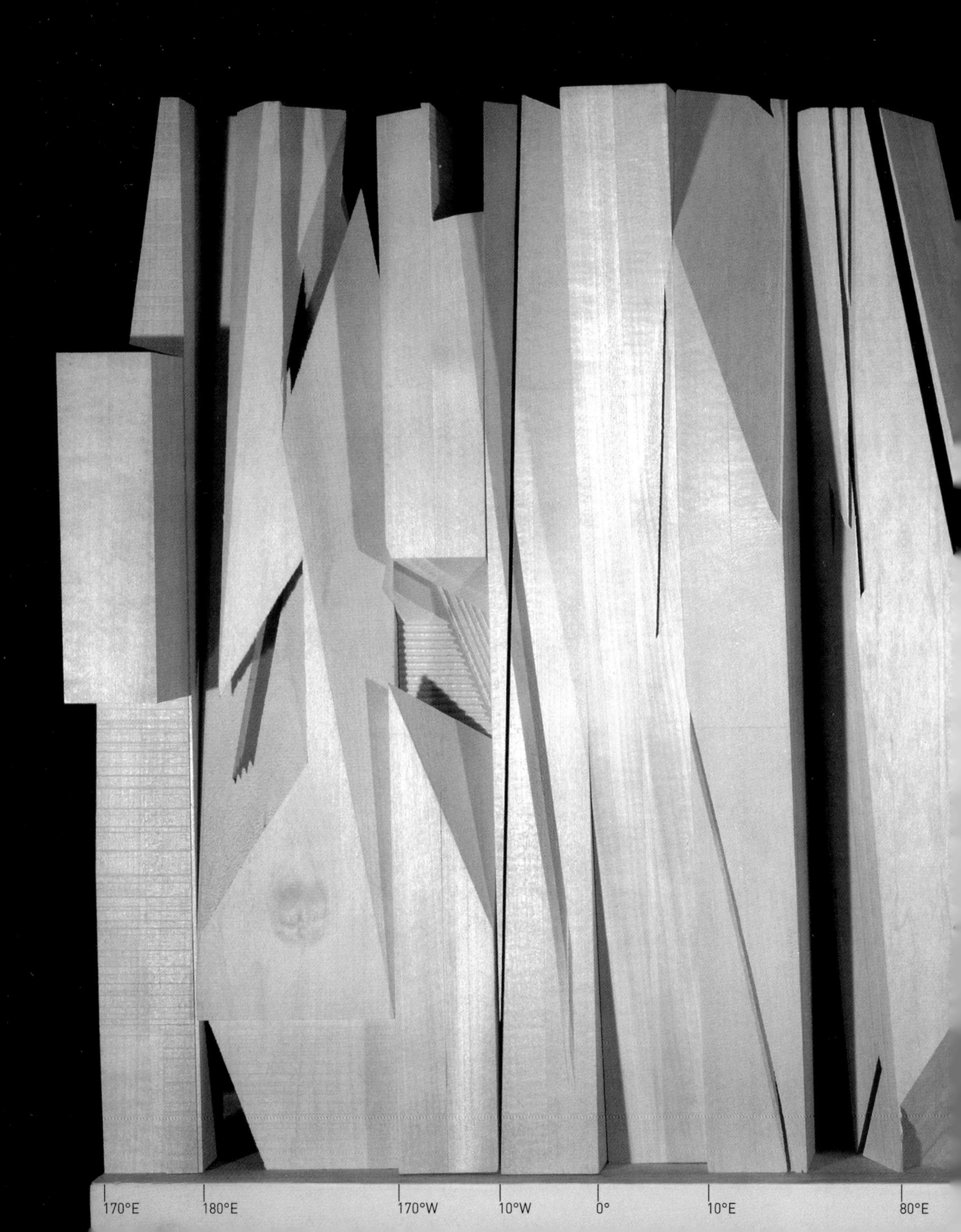

170°E
180°E
170°W
10°W
0°
10°E
80°E

90°W
80°W

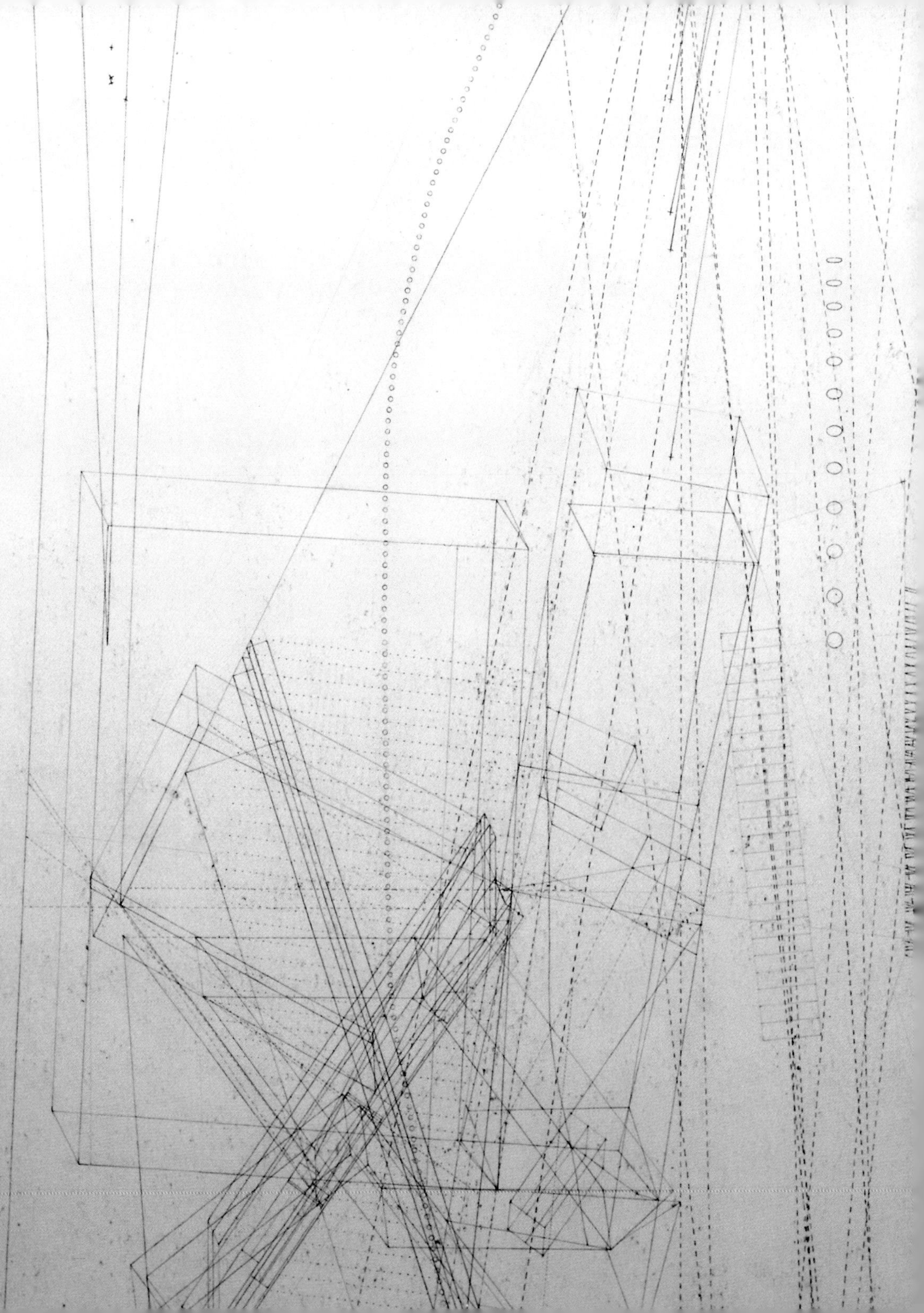

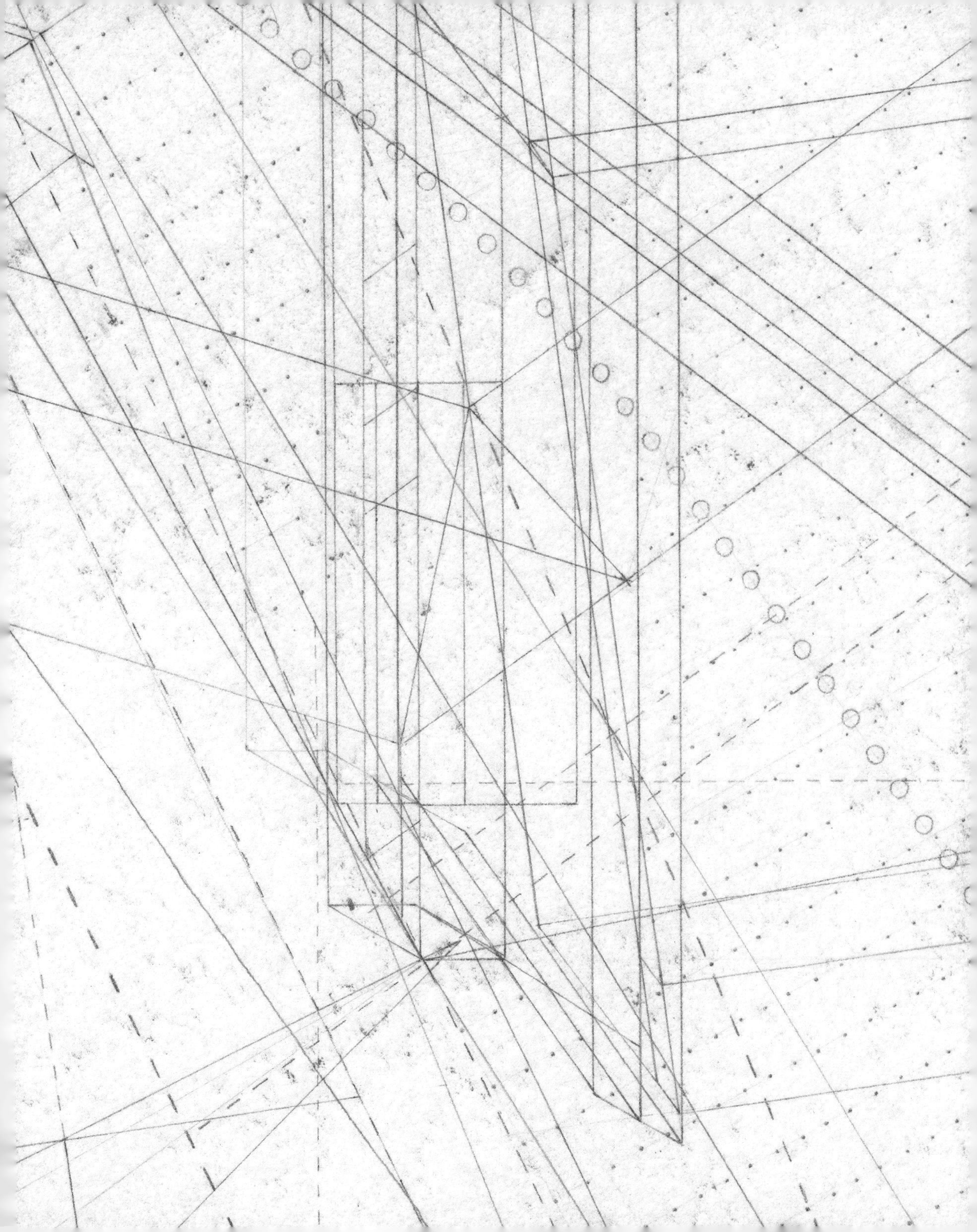

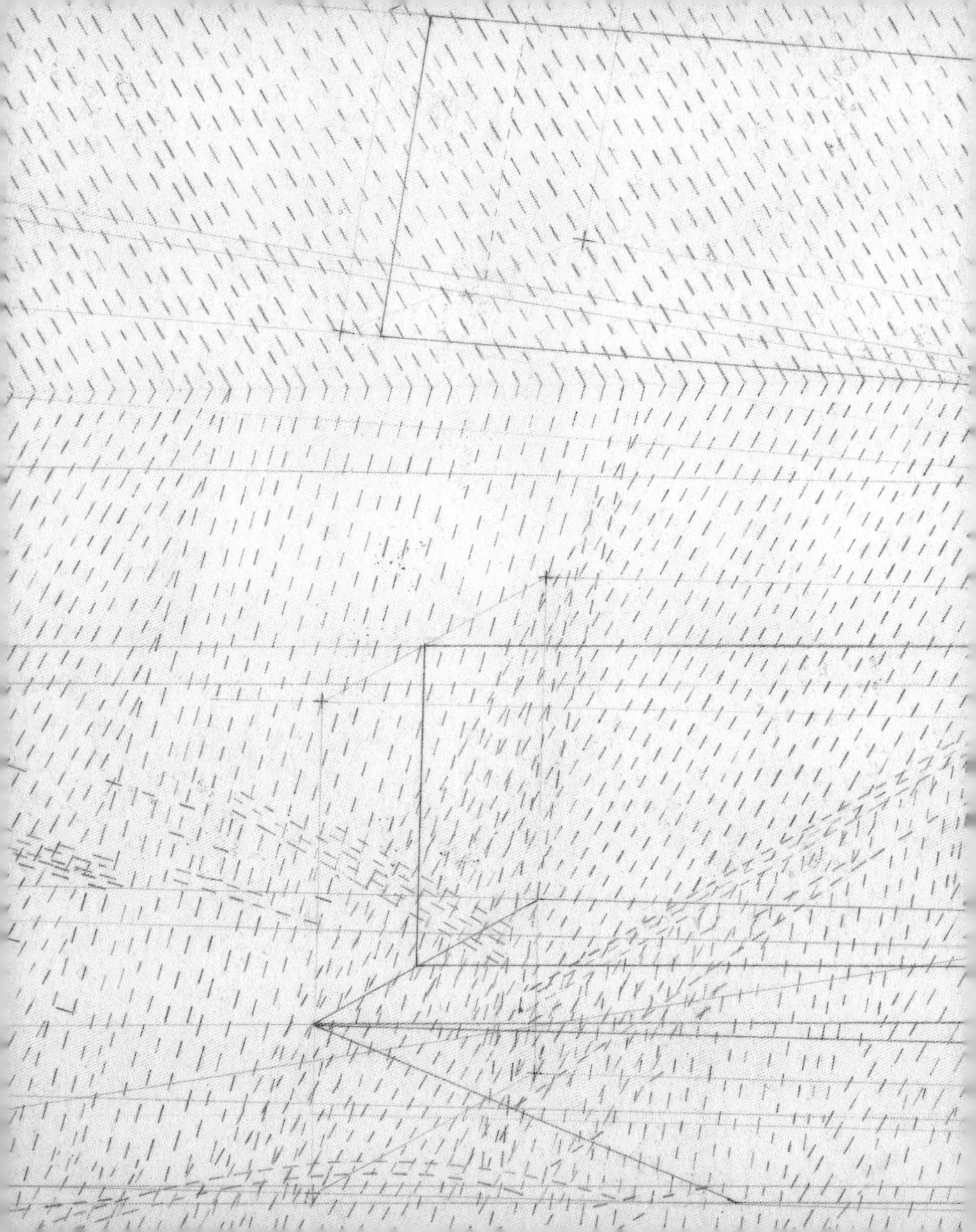

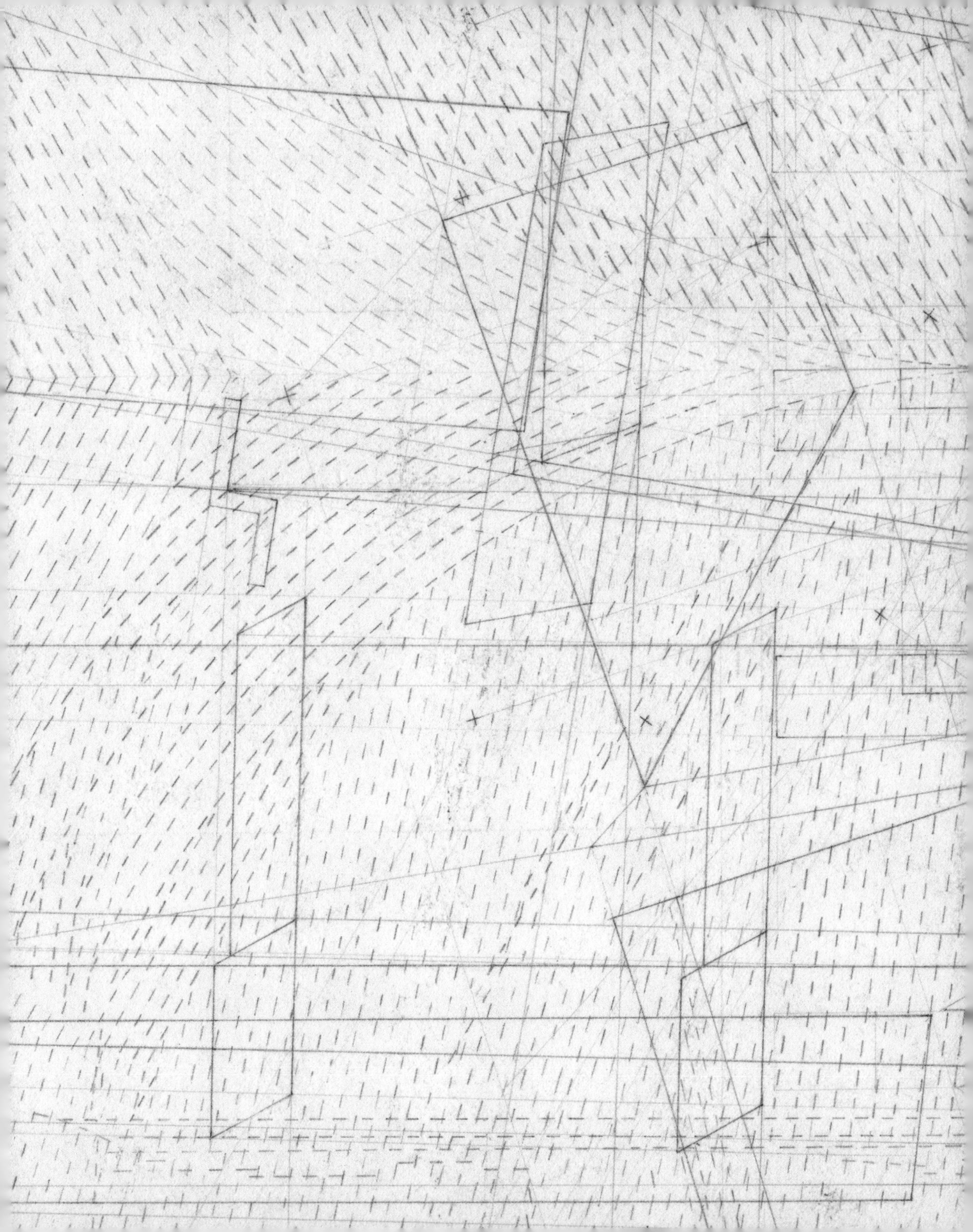

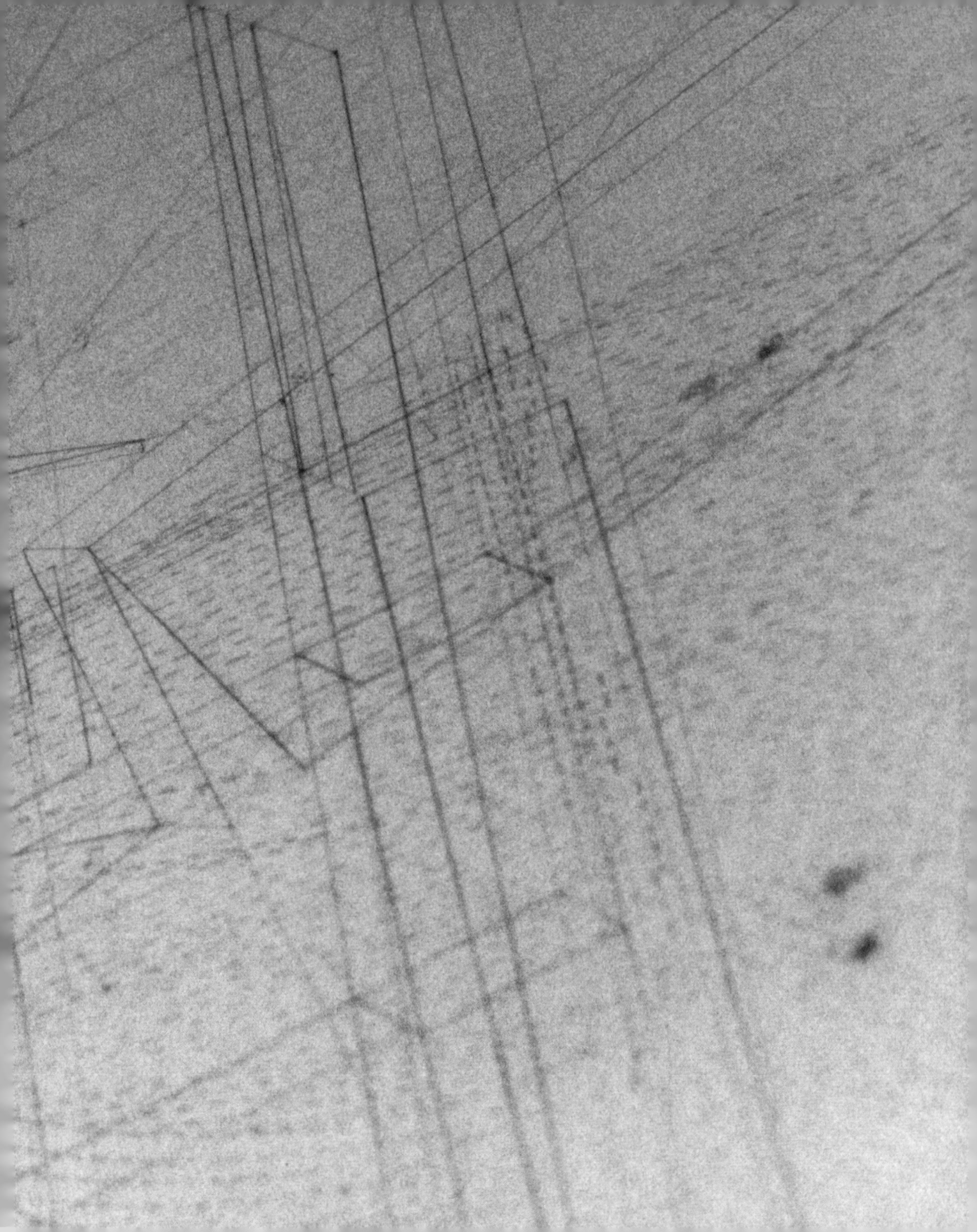

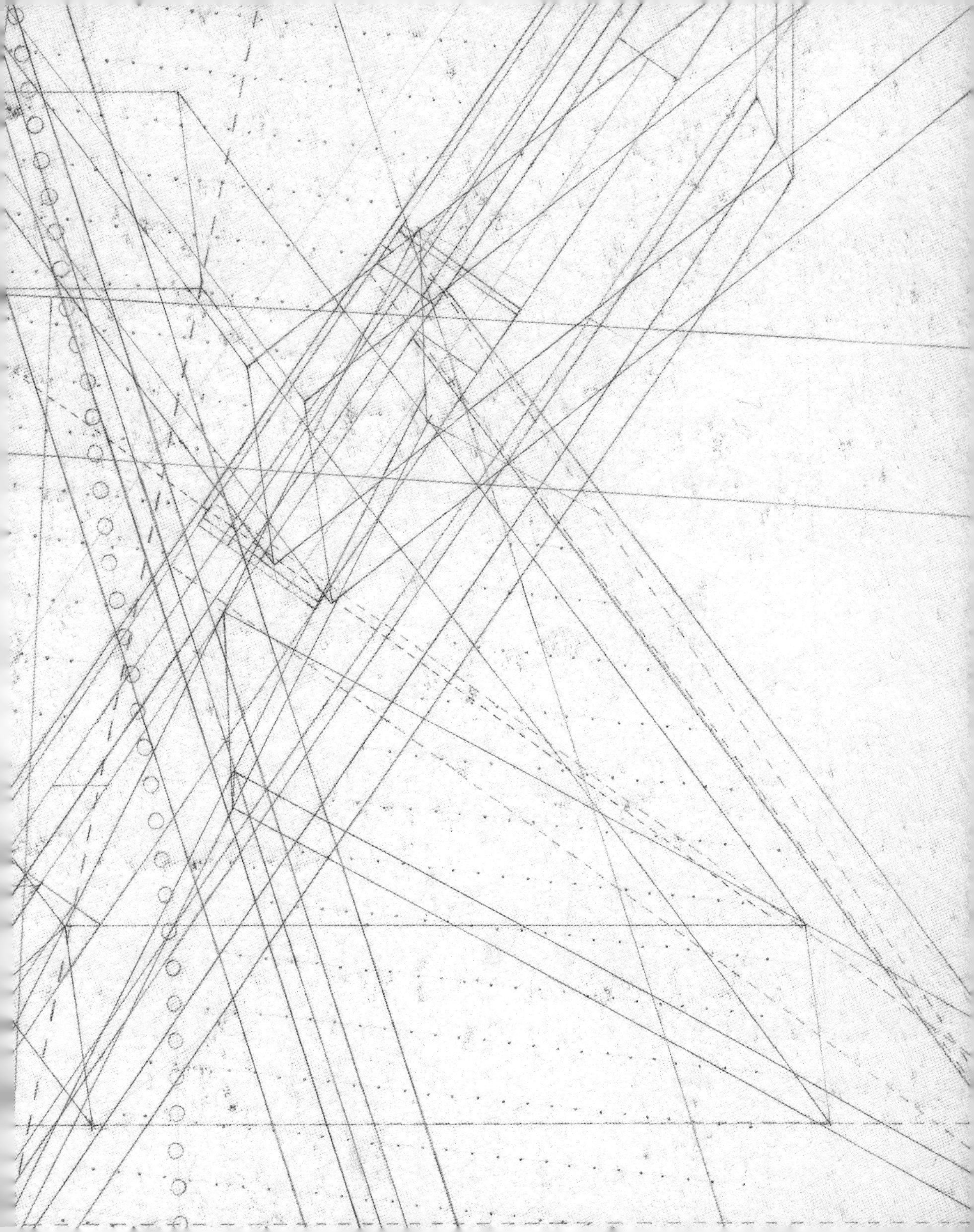

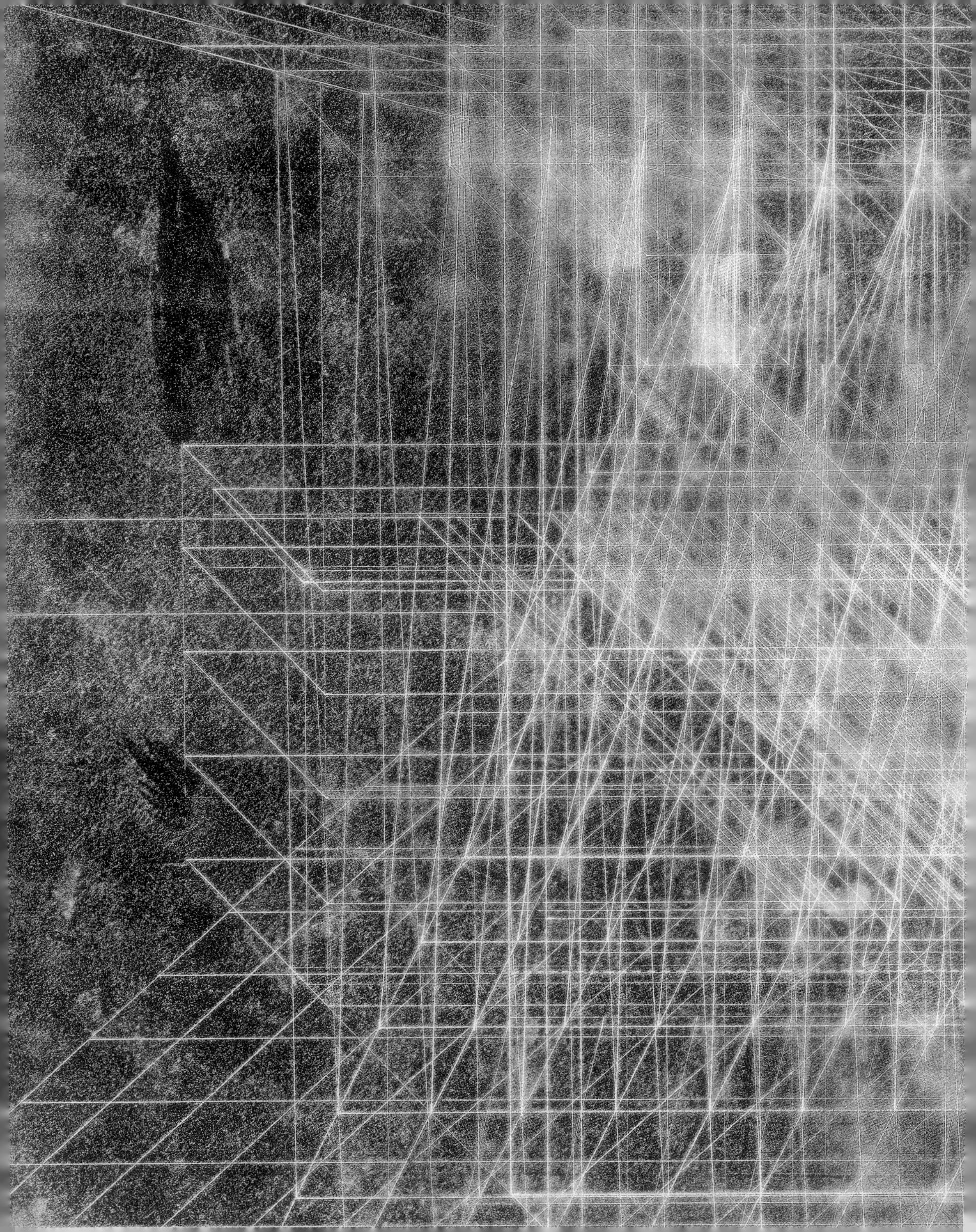